More Than a Pitch-Pipe

THE NEW LAUREL LIBRARY

PETER W. DYKEMA, *General Editor*

More Than a Pitch-Pipe

The HUMAN, PROFESSIONAL, and BUSINESS
RELATIONS of the MUSIC EDUCATOR
to HIS SCHOOL and COMMUNITY

ENNIS DAVIS

C. C. BIRCHARD AND COMPANY
BOSTON · MASSACHUSETTS

Preface

HERE is a book that is different. Usually a text for teachers emanates from a classroom teacher of teachers. While Mr. Davis has frequently spoken to students in educational institutions, that has not been his principal activity. For many years he has travelled throughout our country conferring with superintendents, members of boards of education, principals, supervisors, and teachers.

He has heard and discussed stories of success and of failure. Time after time he has helped to diagnose difficulties and to suggest remedies. He has studied situations from the viewpoints of the children, the parents, the administrators, and the teachers. From these wide personal contacts he has built up a great reservoir of practical wisdom from which he has drawn in preparing the informal talks which form the basis of this book. He has constantly sought to reveal means by which the ambitious teacher can become and remain a valued member of the school staff by making music a vital force in the life of the community. His whimsical title well expresses his conclusions that the successful music educator has been and always must be much more than the blower of a pitchpipe or a sounder of a tuning fork.

The book is personal and practical. It is pleasant to read and easy to remember. No one can study it without applying it to his own work. Filled with homely common sense, interwoven with sound educational principles, it helps greatly in making music teaching a demanding but a rewarding vocation. We have long needed just such a book.

PETER W. DYKEMA
General Editor

v

Foreword

WHAT is security? Is it merely the guarantee of a steady job? Not entirely. It is far more than that. Of greater importance is an inner feeling of confidence and optimism which comes from the assurance that our abilities and talents are well used. An assured livelihood, although important, is secondary to the inner satisfaction which results from work that is mentally, physically, and spiritually exhilarating.

Why do some talented and well-prepared young people fail as music teachers? Generally because of a wrong attitude toward their jobs. They do not accomplish more than routine work. They do not envisage greater aims and finer results. They do not develop in human understanding, tolerance, and the ability to get along with others.

In this book the author creates a design for success in music teaching from which he purposely omits discussion of musicianship and teaching skill—not that musicianship and teaching skill are of lesser importance but because they have been so well and so fully discussed elsewhere. And, strange as it may seem, many of these qualities of greatest importance have seldom been mentioned in our professional literature.

Here are set forth the qualities which we so often have in mind when we say that a music teacher has a "pleasing personality" or is a "live wire." It is emphasized that these qualities can be cultivated the same as the skill to teach or to play an instrument. Too often we assume that people either have or do not have these characteristics just as they possess or do not possess brown eyes, red hair, or freckles. The discussion in this book dispels these mistaken ideas.

This volume for music teachers pictures the interesting business of living with people; of cultivating a greater abundance and variety of human qualities; and of keeping ourselves balanced, cheerful, and normal. Throughout there is implied the faith that the music supervisor who accomplishes these things will be rewarded in the form of an inner joy for a job well done and a life well lived—a reward which would not come to one who would attempt to be merely politically smart or theatrically clever. The reading of this book should give a music teacher a more wholesome and enthusiastic attitude toward life, people, and situations—which, after all, is the key to success, happiness, friendship, and contentment.

The author's statements are based upon many years of first-hand contact with music teaching, music teachers, and school administrators in all parts of the country. His experience as a businessman in music education, as well as a musician and teacher, has given him an opportunity to see these problems more objectively than he could have if his work had been exclusively that of a music teacher and supervisor.

A careful study of this book should be particularly valuable to the beginning teacher who is making his first adjustments to many new situations. Herein the veteran teacher, too, will find many points which he may use in a re-evaluation of his work.

GLENN GILDERSLEEVE

Dover, Delaware
February, 1941

Contents

More Than a Pitch-Pipe

Chapter 1

TEACHING PLUS

Retrospect

FIFTY years ago, say on August 10, 1890, a newspaper story such as the following might have appeared in the Cheltington, Mass., *Sentinel*

Music To Be Taught In Our Schools

INSTRUCTOR FROM NEIGHBORING CITY EMPLOYED BY THE BOARD OF EDUCATION

The board of education has contracted with Mr. Samuel Leamington of the neighboring city of Willston to provide music instruction to the pupils of the Cheltington schools. Mr. Leamington will begin his work here when the schools open on September 6th.

Last night's action by the board of education was taken after the matter had been under official consideration for nearly three months. During that period there has been much discussion of the advisability of introducing the study of music into the schools. Numerous sessions of the board of education have been almost entirely devoted to discussion of the question and many citizens have appeared to make known their attitudes of approval or disapproval.

The final decision was announced after a majority of the board members had become convinced that music instruction rightfully belongs in the school curriculum. A minority group of the board members still contends that all music lessons should be given by private teachers, and that it is not in the province of the public schools and the city treasury to provide instruction other than in the "fundamental" subjects.

Mr. Leamington, the new music teacher, has been organist and choir director at the First Church in Willston during the past six years. He has also served Willston as a private instructor in piano, organ, and voice. His annual inter-church choir festivals and Christmas carol services have been well known and well attended by people of this section of the state. For several years Mr. Leamington has included a large group of children in the annual carol service and it is largely because of his success in training these children that he has been employed by our board of education.

The *Sentinel* believes that the time has come for our schools to offer something more than the usual training in the "three R's." Music instruction is being introduced into a number of schools in our state and throughout the country, and we believe that our board of education is justified in taking this step forward even though we realize that many of our citizens and taxpayers are not yet entirely convinced of the wisdom of the course.

Congratulations and good wishes, Mr. Leamington!

1

On the morning of September 6, 1892, Samuel Leamington walked resolutely and anxiously toward the entrance of the Longfellow School. Pupils lined the walk and silently watched him pass. Teachers inside the building caught glimpses of him from behind half-concealing curtains. Pupils and teachers were saying to themselves and to each other "There's the new music teacher."

In his coat pocket Samuel carried a pitch-pipe. Under his arm was a package containing a staff-liner and a music chart. Those three items constituted the complete equipment for the music instruction program of the Cheltington Schools and, incidentally, all three of them belonged to Samuel rather than to the schools.

Samuel had no courses of study. He had spent no time in college classes having to do with curriculum making, psychology of music, methods, and supervision. His training had been that of a practical and practicing musician rather than that of a teacher. Indeed, he would have been hard put to find professional *music education* training at that time and probably would have had to secure it from individuals rather than in normal schools and colleges.

What did Samuel do in the Cheltington Schools? He taught singing—from room to room, from building to building, day after day. His methods were probably of the kind which we would call "formal" today. But let's not concern ourselves with Samuel's classroom procedures. The important thing is that his lean, hard-fibered curriculum of singing and sight-reading provided the first step in the history of music in the Cheltington schools. Let no one think that his job was an easy one just because he did not have to provide training in eurhythmics, wind and string instruments, piano classes, theory, appreciation, creative activities, and the like. He did not have so many different things to do, but his was a pioneer's job in a community and in a school system where citizens, teachers, and pupils were generally unconvinced that music had a rightful place in public education. Nor could Samuel depend upon effective and smooth-working music education programs of surrounding communities to influence the attitude of the Cheltington people. His nearest fellow teacher in school music was sixty miles away.

Although he had been employed primarily as a musician it turned out that Samuel was a really good *teacher* and it was as a teacher that he functioned, not as a supervisor. There was very little for him to worry about so far as management and organization were concerned. His daily routine of teaching was his own and it was easy for him to plan.

During the twenty-two years of Samuel's service in Cheltington (1890-1912) he built a fine foundation for and erected a part of the structure of music education as it exists there today. He had strength of character. He taught thousands of pupils to sing and helped them to master notation. His strenuous program of sight-singing brought forth high school choruses which gave fine performances of great music, performances which the older Cheltington people remember to this day.

Toward the end of Samuel's tenure, music education began to increase in scope. Samuel once formed a small orchestra but it was not highly successful. He established a theory class in high school and did a good job with it even though the enrollment was small. But the more elaborate program which Cheltington follows today was not for his time.

We salute Samuel for his vision, his capacity for hard work, his intense sincerity, and his many contributions to the community and the schools through music.

Today

Henry Walters* had a visitor this morning. Henry is now the supervisor of music in Cheltington. He was working quietly in the music office in the new high school building when a voice said, "Do you mind if I come in and talk with you a while?"

Henry looked up but saw no one.

The voice continued, "I am the spirit of Samuel Leamington. Once upon a time I taught music here in the Cheltington schools and I thought I would come back to see how the work which I started is coming along. By the way, I *do* appreciate your hanging my picture in your new office. I used to worry a lot about it when it was hanging behind the door of the little backstage alcove of the assembly hall in the old high school building. You know that alcove was the nearest thing to office quarters I ever had.

"And was it difficult for me to locate you and your office! This building is so large that I can hardly find my way around. My, my, how different it is from our old high school building."

Henry had never before carried on a conversation with a spirit and he felt more than a little ill at ease. He pushed a chair in the direction from which the voice seemed to come.

"Sit down, Mr. Leamington. I'm glad to have an opportunity to talk with you because I have heard so many people here in town tell about the 'good old days' when you taught music here and how much they enjoyed singing for you."

"Thank you, my boy. I'm glad to know that my work made some lasting impressions, though I used to wonder whether I was accomplishing much."

*All names, locations, and situations in this volume are wholly fictitious. There is no reference to real characters or to actual events.

After slight hesitation Mr. Leamington's voice continued, "I've been following you in your work during the past several days without your knowing it and I thought you might like to hear what I think about the way things are being done."

"I certainly should, Mr. Leamington."

"Well, you have led me a merry chase. Music teaching was never like this in my day. I'm practically exhausted after trailing you for several days."

"But, Mr. Leamington, I've been on my regular schedule. The last few days have been no different from my work all through the year. Look at my schedule here and you will see that I have been following it as usual."

"Yes, I know, but I don't see how you manage to do all these things. Why, you rush from band rehearsal to grade teaching to choir rehearsal to piano classes to operetta rehearsal to appreciation classes to radio performances, and so on all day and sometimes well into the night."

Henry laughed. "It *is* rather a hard job to keep up to my schedule on some days. I don't suppose that you had so many things to take care of in your time."

"I should say not! When I started teaching music here no one expected me to do anything more than teach singing and sight-reading. I don't know what people would have thought if I had tried to start a lot of the work that is in your everyday program now."

"Well, Mr. Leamington, I don't mind telling you that it is difficult for me to keep so many different music activities under way. This music education field has been branching out and a young fellow has to do a lot of work to be well informed about the new ideas and methods. And knowing music and how to teach it isn't all that concerns me. I have quite a problem in the management and organization of my work."

"There, my boy, you've said something. I like the way that you go about your work. You seem to know what you are doing and you know how to plan with real efficiency. Of course, in my day I just taught classes nearly all the time and I didn't have a lot of your problems."

Mr. Leamington continued, "What is more, you have taken your work and yourself into the community. I used to direct a choir in one of the churches here, but school music was kept pretty well inside the schools except for an occasional public performance. Now your work seems to spread right out into the community all the time. I've been watching you as you walk down the street. Everyone in town knows you. Everyone who speaks to you seems to think that you are making music do something for *him*."

"Thanks, Mr. Leamington. I'm glad to hear you say that. By the way, while you are here I'd like to ask your advice on a teaching problem. The other day when I was teaching a fifth grade class I had a lot of trouble with two rhythm problems and I . . ."

"Yes, Henry, I know. I was right there when it happened and I must say that you didn't seem to know just what to do. Now let me tell you how I used to teach those problems. In the first place you . . ."

We leave them with their conversation and comparison of notes.

Contrast

Yes, the job that Henry Walters has today is very different from the one which Samuel Leamington had some decades ago. How it has grown! What added responsibilities!

Mr. Leamington was a good teacher. So is Henry. Mr. Leamington was a good musician. So is Henry. But in addition to his being a good teacher and a good musician Henry must also be skillful and tactful in his human, professional, and business relations to his school and his community.

When Henry walks out of the front door of a school building he isn't leaving his job behind. His music program does not recognize the boundaries of school walls. His work does not begin at eight-thirty and end at three. Culture does not grow just at certain spots and at certain times. Henry wants music to be an ever-present factor in the daily life of Cheltington rather than a mere school "subject" which is automatically turned on and off by the master clock which controls the bell system in the schools.

Let's look at Henry's schedule for today. First, we see his regular classes and rehearsals—and they make up a rather full day's work. But what are these "extra" duties which he has listed? Let's read them:

Talk with fifth grade teachers about new social studies units.
Discuss next year's budget figures with superintendent.
Write state chairman about contest entries.
Read proof at printer's for Thursday evening concert program.
See Brewster School principal about piano classes.
Test new clarinets which dealer has stocked.
Check next week's Rotary program with chairman.
Order new choir music.
Send for Eastern University Summer School bulletin.
Have bull fiddle repaired.

Are these "extras"? Not at all. These duties are an essential part of the development of Henry's program to make music more important in the lives of the Cheltington pupils and their families. They must be taken care of—and efficiently too.

So goes the daily life of Henry Walters and of many other supervisors who have raised their music education programs from the level of classroom routine to that of energetic and penetrating community activity.

Where is Henry likely to encounter the greatest number of his daily problems?. In his own musical and pedagogical adequacy? In his classroom and rehearsal techniques? No. He will meet most of them in the business of shaping and fitting his program to the daily lives of pupils, teaching staff, and community.

Many of these problems will not be truly musical or pedagogical in nature. They will be problems of management, organization, and business. What is more important, nearly all of them will have underlying *human* implications and connections because they will have to do with the everyday living of many people in the schools and in the community. Henry cannot plan his work simply to suit himself. Regardless of his superior musicianship and teaching ability he must keep himself highly aware of and sensitive to the effect which his plans will have on other people.

It seems entirely safe to say that a large majority of young supervisors who fail of reappointment to their positions do so because of lack of general efficiency in management and organization and disregard for necessary personal adjustment to surrounding factors and influences.

How many case histories could be written of the failure of supervisors who have possessed good musicianship and good teaching ability! In many instances these "failures" have been temporary, and the experience gained in one situation has taught the supervisor what to do and what not to do in his next position. However, this is an expensive and dangerous form of education.

Many times we have heard school administrators say something like this, "This man who is teaching music for us seems to be a good musician. He plays the piano pretty well and has a pleasant voice. He has done good work with the band and has started a choir. But . . .."

And then come the reasons why a music supervisor is going to lose his job. Will those reasons deal with the individual's musical or pedagogical inadequacy? Not often. Then why is he losing his job? In most instances because of lack of insight into human relations, maladjustment to community life and habits, friction with the structure and authority of the school system, general inefficiency, or personal shortcomings.

Caution!

Let no one interpret the foregoing statements as a thesis that the successful music supervisor is primarily an intelligent businessman with a flair for public relations.

It is not in the province of this volume to treat the content, structure, and procedures of the music education curriculum.

It is considered axiomatic that a good music educator is essentially a competent and sensitive musician; that he has thorough professional interest and intent; that his professional training has been adequate; and that his ideals are well founded upon a true conception of music as an art.

If the following chapters seem to be heavily flavored with pragmatism it is because of deliberate intent—and with the belief that the professional literature of music education has provided all too brief treatment of the practical problems of music supervision while at the same time it has furnished a wealth of material having to do with the philosophical and psychological aspects of music and music education.

Chapter 2

SECURING A POSITION

LET'S step in and listen to a conversation which is going on in the lobby of a hotel where a meeting of music educators is being held.

"Hello, Jack!"

"Hi'ya, Tim! How's everything?"

"Fine. How is it with you? Haven't seen you since we left college."

"That's right—and it's beginning to seem like a long time ago. Are you still teaching the kids in Rushton how to toot horns?"

"In Rushton? No. I left there two years ago. I'm down at Monmouth now. Much better job. Got a nice increase in salary, too. Are you still at Midland?"

"No. I left Midland last year. I'm at Livingston now. You know, near Morton where Phil Harmon is teaching."

"Is Phil at Morton now? I thought he was still located in Leeland. When did he move?"

"Oh, about two years ago. He's got a grand set-up over there now in that big new central school. Say! Someone told me that Hugh Fortner is here. Have you seen him?"

"No, I haven't. But I understand he got that good job that opened up in Lancaster last fall. Old Hugh always did know how to get in the front row."

"Harry Kechney was here just a minute ago and was telling me about his new plan for beginning instrumental classes. I think he has a good idea. It's like this . . .."

Two days later we look in on the same meeting. Here is Paul Lewis. He has just checked out of the hotel and is starting home to Cartersville where he has been teaching music ever since he graduated from college in the same class with Jack, Tim, Phil, and Hugh.

Paul isn't in a good humor at all. In fact, he is rather disgusted with the whole business of music education. He's wondering why he didn't have sense enough to become a lawyer, a doctor, a . . . oh, well, anything but a music teacher.

What's the trouble with Paul? Well, he has been talking with the other boys who were his close friends in college. He has heard them tell of their advancements. He knows that all of them have moved into better and larger positions which command higher salaries while he has remained in the same position in Cartersville and his salary today is little more than it was when he started there.

Paul knows that when he was in college he was just as good a musician as Jack and the rest of them. His grades were just as good. He was as active in campus affairs as they. But they have gone ahead while he has been standing still.

If we were to talk to Paul's former instructors they would tell us that he was just as capable and industrious as the other members of his class. If we were to go to Cartersville today we should find that Paul is doing a good job there. But Cartersville is a small town with limited resources. Paul knows, better than anyone else, that Cartersville does not offer him much opportunity for further advancement.

Paul has wanted a new position for a long time. The other boys have been moving into better jobs. Why can't he? In the first place, Paul is a fellow who has a peculiar line of thinking which makes him feel that someone should come along and seek him out for a new job. After all, he says to

himself, his college record was good and his work in Cartersville has been successful. Why shouldn't someone recognize
these things and come after him?

Because of this attitude Paul has never bothered to study
the techniques of obtaining positions. Several times the college from which he was graduated has suggested his name for
new positions. But in each instance he bungled things and his
application received no serious consideration. Superintendents of schools in several larger surrounding towns know of
him and his work but they do not think of him as a likely
candidate when they have positions to fill. So far as they are
concerned he just doesn't have the right approach toward
the business of getting a new job.

They Do Move Around

The annual turn-over of positions in music education is
said to be relatively one of the largest in the entire field of
education. In the offices of the Music Educators National
Conference are rows of cabinets which contain the names and
addresses of thousands of music instructors in all parts of the
country. A staff of skilled workers is required to keep those
files up to date and to enter the names of newcomers and the
changes of addresses of those who are moving from one position to another.

We shall not debate here whether music educators are too
restless and too "perigrinatious" for their own good and for
the good of the cause of music education. It is sufficient for
our purpose to know that at all times the problem of finding
a position occupies an important place in the minds of several
thousand people who are concerned about securing their
first positions or who are anxious to change.

Paul Lewis looks upon music education as a profession. It is. But when it comes time for him to try for a position he is really in *business*—the business of selling his services. Let him not lull himself into complacency and inactivity or be haughty because of an idea that he is a "professional" person who has no need to take good care of his own business problems.

Evaluation

Before we consider the mechanics of securing positions we may well weigh the relative values' of "small" and "large" jobs.

The size of the population of a town or city is not indicative of the opportunities for music education which exist there. Smaller communities, particularly those remote from urban areas, many times offer the most fertile fields.

The larger the school system the more remote the supervisor is likely to be from the actual teaching of music; the greater will be his involvement in desk and routine work; and the more numerous will be the "headaches" which are inherent in the administration of the affairs of many people.

The supervisor who wishes to keep close to the lives of young people and who finds his greatest joy in teaching may do well to stay in a smaller position.

The supervisor who likes the feel of close community relationships and who wishes to know his neighbors well will be happier in the smaller community.

Some of the most distinguished careers in music education have been founded and developed in the small or medium-sized town.

Size does not necessarily indicate importance or success.

Avenues of Information

College and university placement bureaus. In some institutions these bureaus handle all correspondence and negotiations in recommending student candidates for positions and rely upon members of the music education faculty for advice and counsel. In other schools the head of the music education department or some other staff member may have the principal responsibility. In any case, the graduating student must depend to a great extent upon his college record for recommendations for his first position.

If, during his four years at Central University, Sam Williams has made a good scholastic record; been alert and conscientious in his work; continued to develop favorable personal traits, including good manners; shown some spark of real professional interest in music education; and convinced faculty and students that he is capable and deserving, he may rest assured that everyone on the college staff will help him in every way possible to secure his first position. If his record is a generally unfavorable one—well, it is difficult to figure just how Sam is going to get a good start. Perhaps he should have changed over to some other field of training a long time ago. But, let's assume that Sam is worthy of good recommendation and that his college assists him in a successful search for his first position. When he begins teaching he must keep some facts about the future in the back of his mind.

The music education faculty members at Central University are interested in the success of the students to whom they have given training. They appreciate occasional letters from their former students telling of triumphs and troubles, progress and problems. They like to think that Sam and his classmates are appreciative of the training given to them at

Central. Sam gets a thrill when his pupils give him credit for their training. Well, why shouldn't Sam's former teachers be pleased to learn that he is doing some worth-while things and that he gives them some of the credit?

Many school administrators ask training schools to recommend experienced supervisors as well as new graduates. When such requests are received it is perfectly natural for members of the music education faculty to think first of those students about whose work they have received reports since the time of their graduation. So, if Sam is looking intelligently toward the future he will make certain that the faculty at Central hears of his activities. He need not write long accounts of woe and misery or overly confident letters which give the impression of great self-satisfaction, but rather some brief, friendly letters which tell honestly of his progress. If he will send printed programs of his concerts, operettas, and other performances they will probably be posted on the bulletin board, thereby showing the present student body what a former graduate is accomplishing.

The faculty members at Central will place several good marks to Sam's future credit if he will notify them of available music positions in towns surrounding his teaching location. He helps Central—Central helps him.

Teachers agencies. It is the business of teachers agencies to help candidates find the right jobs and to help school administrators find the right people for available positions. Reputable agencies are conscientious in the matter of recommendations. They wish to establish good records of service with administrators so that their recommendations may have professional and business values comparable to the satisfactory services of a physician, a lawyer, or a teacher, or the products of any reputable business firm. If an agency makes a poor recommendation to an administrator he may hesitate to return to it for further dealings.

An agency spends much time, money, and effort in the collection of information about existing vacancies. It carefully goes through the files of its enrolled members to find those people who are best qualified for the positions at hand. It does thorough investigating for the hiring administrator. It earns and deserves the fee that is paid to it.

It should be observed that the ethical code of the National Association of Teachers Agencies provides that "Candidates known to be unfit shall not be recommended. Notices of vacancies shall not be sent without definite knowledge that such vacancies exist. It shall be the policy of the association that candidates be recommended upon direct call from school officials." Information about vacancies received from a teachers agency is of a strictly confidential nature. It is unethical to give it to others.

If Sam Williams receives from an agency a notification of a vacancy about which he has previously been informed through other channels he should immediately inform the agency and do so in a way which will convince the agency that its notification was not the first.

It is both courteous and businesslike to acknowledge all notifications sent by agencies. An agency is in a much better position to be of service to a candidate if it knows what action the candidate has taken on notifications which have been sent to him.

Some agencies have special departments for the placement of music teachers, others exist solely for that purpose, and still others make no special efforts in that direction. Some agencies are geographically widespread in their coverage and others specialize in certain limited territories. A list of the members of the National Association of Teachers Agencies and their addresses is included on pages 173-75.

Individuals. Sam Williams has now been in his first position for three years. He wants to move into a better one with more opportunities and more salary. In addition to soliciting help from his Alma Mater's placement bureau and a teachers agency he does some correspondence on his own initiative. His college classmates are scattered over a wide area. Some friendly (but not too obvious) correspondence with them may bring information about the very kind of position for which he is looking.

Sam has attended several professional meetings and conferences during his three years of teaching. He has met a number of supervisors and directors from larger towns and cities, also some school administrators. He has had opportunity to talk with them and exchange ideas—and he may have found his next position through one of these conversations. *He did not make the error of giving the impression that he had attended these meetings for the principal purpose of making contacts for a new job.*

Applying for the Right Position

Willie Blount is a perpetual applicant. If he hears that there is going to be a vacancy anywhere he applies for the job. From Maine to California; from kindergarten through college; from toy orchestra to symphony; from rote songs to opera—everything is in Willie's range, that is, according to his way of thinking. He just wants a new job. It would never occur to him to make some inquiry about the nature of a position and its particular requirements before he makes an application. He sits down and writes the same old application letter to everyone, and everyone, upon receiving the letter recognizes the characteristics of the habitual "applier."

P.S. Willie doesn't get the jobs.

In Person or in Writing?

A recent survey shows that more than 4000 college graduates are granted music education degrees every year. More than 200 colleges, universities, and conservatories which are well scattered throughout the country grant these degrees. The supply of music supervisors on the market is sufficiently large and well distributed that most administrators can easily assemble a group of candidates for *personal* interviews when they wish to fill a vacancy. Because of this condition it is becoming more and more difficult for the candidate to secure positions by means of correspondence only. Most administrators insist upon seeing and talking with applicants whom they are seriously considering for positions. If negotiations must be carried on by mail there is great need for the applicant to have the seconding of strong recommending agencies of one kind or another.

The personal interview is strongly recommended regardless of how initial information concerning the vacancy may have been obtained.

The Personal Application

Preliminary investigation. Jim McArthur has heard that there is a music job waiting for someone in Williamsburg. If his information has been received from the placement bureau of the college from which he was graduated or from a teachers agency, he probably knows the nature of the work involved—

whether it is a general supervisorship, a grade school position, a high school position, an instrumental position, etc. If he has heard about it in a roundabout manner he may know nothing of the details. Let's assume the latter. Now instead of sitting down and writing a regular letter of application he writes to the superintendent of schools at Williamsburg in the following manner:

JAMES MCARTHUR

221 PINE RIDGE ROAD

WINTON, N. J.

June 15, 1941

Mr. Walter Jones
Superintendent of Schools
Williamsburg, N. J.

Dear Mr. Jones:

I have recently learned of a music vacancy in your schools, but do not have any details concerning it. If it is the kind of position for which I am qualified I should like to make formal application.

Will you kindly advise me whether this position is a general supervisorship or specialized work in elementary school or high school, vocal or instrumental. Enclosed is a stamped return envelope.

Very truly yours,

James McArthur

Jim very rightly believes that Mr. Jones may consider him a rather conscientious fellow from the outset because he is trying to make certain that he will apply for only the kind of job for which he is competent.

Jim has figured ahead of time that he will be writing some letters in his search for a position, so he has spent two dollars on printed letterheads. He writes the first draft of his letters in longhand, and since his ability at the typewriter is somewhat limited he has a friend make the final copy. He knows that when Mr. Jones looks over his morning's mail he likes to read the neatly typewritten letters before he reads the others.

Making an appointment. A few days later Mr. Jones writes his reply and Jim sees that the job is just the kind for which he is qualified. Of course he can sit down and write another letter asking for an appointment, but he thinks that other applicants may be busily after the job and he wants some quick action, so he steps to the telephone and calls Mr. Jones by long distance and asks him if he may come for a personal interview. The date is set.

More investigation. Jim has never been in Williamsburg but he does not wait until he arrives there to find out something about the town and its schools. He goes down to his home town public library and secures a directory which gives facts and statistics about New Jersey towns. He digs out all the information he can about Williamsburg's size, its principal resources and industries, and something of its history. He then goes to the high school and asks the principal if he will look in the state educational directory and give him all the information possible about the Williamsburg school system— the number of teachers, the size of the high school enrollment, the number of elementary schools, etc. During the next few days he makes inquiries among his friends and among the businessmen in Winton as to what they know about Williamsburg. Among other things, he finds that his Uncle Henry knows a druggist, Mr. Kermit, in Williamsburg, and it later turns out that Mr. Kermit is on the board of education.

When Jim arrives in Williamsburg he already knows enough about it that things seem familiar to him. He makes a point of arriving about two hours before his appointment and spends some time looking around the town. When he goes in to see Mr. Jones he feels more or less at home.

The interview. Here we come to an unpredictable situation, one regarding which it is very difficult to offer advice and counsel. To forecast the direction which an interview will take is impossible. Two personalities have to work out that problem face to face.

Shall Jim take the initiative and try to sell himself to Mr. Jones right off and run the risk of having Mr. Jones think that he is too forward? Or, shall he wait for Mr. Jones to direct the conversation and limit himself to answering questions and risk having Mr. Jones think that he is lacking in force and self-assertion?

When Mr. Jones looks up from his desk as Jim enters his office he is going to make up his mind very quickly on a number of points—even before Jim says a single word. What kind of a general appearance does this fellow make? Is his carriage erect and alert? Does he walk with poise and purpose or does he shuffle and hesitate? Does his face express life and vitality or does it lack animation? Is his grooming neat and in good taste or is he unkempt and perhaps arrayed in some of last year's most startling examples of campus design in haberdashery? Does he have a pleasant speaking voice and does he know how to greet people on first meeting? Does he have a firm handshake or is it flabby?

If we are honest at this point we may as well admit that many interviews are over before they start. Mr. Jones and other administrators must keep certain questions in the foreground even before they start to investigate technical qualifications. How would this fellow appear on the stage before a high school assembly? What kind of an impression would he make in a talk or in a performance before a community organization? How would the citizens of the community react to his personality? Does he appear capable of leadership?

Jim isn't handsome. He wouldn't go far in a Hollywood screen test. That isn't important. His clothes do not look expensive. That isn't expected of him. But they are clothes which are in good taste for a business interview—not sports clothes. His suit is well pressed and his shoes are shined. In general, his appearance and his manners indicate an intelligent and alert young man with good taste and good manners, and with a purpose in view.

Jim doesn't know it but one of his former classmates, Muriel Conrad, was here yesterday making application for the same position. When she entered the door Mr. Jones took just one look at her and that was enough. Why did she over-emphasize her make-up? Her rather sloppy combination of sports clothes with an abundance of costume jewelry certainly did not make her appear to best advantage. When she placed her hands on the desk at one time during the interview Mr. Jones observed her brilliantly polished nails and her fingers yellowed with cigarette stains. Muriel just wasted time in making the trip.

Beginning with some casual talk about the weather and Jim's drive from Winton to Williamsburg the interview soon gets down to business. Mr. Jones wants to know about Jim's training and experience. They discuss his general education and his professional music education. What about his performing ability in singing or playing in public? Is he interested in community activities? What are his views on the development of good bands and orchestras? How does he make out in the supervising of grade teachers? Could he develop a good choir in the high school? And so on and on. Jim has brought his instrument and some music with him so that he is ready for a demonstration of his performing ability in case Mr. Jones asks him to sing or play.

During this interview Jim is looking Mr. Jones squarely in the eye, sitting easily and comfortably (but not slouchily) in his chair, keeping his voice clear and well modulated and thinking just as fast as he can. He speaks with conviction but does not give the impression of being over-confident or dogmatic.

As the discussion continues Jim is constantly feeding into it all the facts and figures which he has already learned about Williamsburg. He does this so well that Mr. Jones finally asks him if he has ever been here before. Jim says not. Mr. Jones says he seems to know a lot about the town and its school. This is the opportunity for which Jim has been waiting and off he goes:

"Mr. Jones, if I came to Williamsburg to teach I wouldn't want to feel like an outsider who is here just to do a job and draw a salary. I'd want to consider myself a part of the community and its life. I've spent some time looking up information about Williamsburg and its schools. This morning I spent two hours driving through different parts of the town to get acquainted with it. I shouldn't want to make application to you for this music position unless I thought I should really be happy living and working here and making myself a part of the community."

Mr. Jones has interviewed a great many candidates for positions in his experience as superintendent of schools. In years past when he was a teacher he sat on the other side of the desk where Jim is now sitting. He knows how it feels, and he is quite likely to guide the conversation so that Jim will have the best possible opportunity to present himself favorably.

Before Jim leaves he will hand to Mr. Jones a carefully prepared outline of his training and experience accompanied by a photograph of himself. Mr. Jones will then not have to remember all the things which Jim has told him about himself or rely on the very sketchy notes which he has been taking during the interview. He appreciates this thoughtfulness on Jim's part because he can now easily give all facts to board of education members from Jim's typewritten outline* and can also show Jim's picture which is, by the way, a really good one, not just a cheap one which would probably make him look rather foolish. Distorted and unreal looking photographs have cost many candidates their opportunities for positions.

Incidentally, it is interesting to note that Jim has provided a well-considered list of references—his former superintendent of schools, his former high school principal, the head of the music department in the college from which he was graduated, and a minister in his home town. Those four men are in position to present a good evaluation of Jim's personal background, his professional training, and his success as a teacher and community worker.

When Mr. Jones has secured all the information he wishes to have he will thank Jim for coming to see him and will tell him that the matter will be decided within the next week or so and that he still has some other candidates to interview. Jim goes home feeling both better and worse at the same time. Did he do everything just right? Did he say the right things? Did he make a good appearance or was his tie (which seemed to be a very subdued one at college last year) a little on the

*Jim's outline of his training and experience is found on page 176.

"loud" side in a school office? Did he talk too much or too little? He will debate these and many other questions on the way home and for some days to come.

We hope he gets the job.

Application by Letter

Lucy Hunter has been recommended by a teachers agency for a position that is nearly two thousand miles from her home. Mr. Hanks, the superintendent of schools in Vistula, Washington, has been looking for a music instructor who can supervise grade school music, direct a good a cappella choir in high school, and organize beginning class piano instruction. Candidates having exactly the qualifications for that combination of work seem few and far between. Mr. Hanks has not succeeded in finding a likely candidate who is located near him and he has become very much interested in the information about Lucy which has been sent to him by the Universal Teachers Agency.

Lucy would like to have this job. It pays a good salary, and she has always wanted to live in the northwest. But here she is two thousand miles away in her home town of Dexter, Alabama. She doesn't have the money to make the trip to Washington State solely for the purpose of making a personal application, no matter how much she wants the job. Mr. Hanks is pretty sure she would be the right person for the position but he knows that the Vistula Board of Education will not pay Lucy's expenses for a trip from Alabama to Washington for a personal interview.

It looks as if they are going to have to settle the matter by correspondence. Let's take a look at Lucy's first letter to Mr. Hanks.

LUCY HUNTER
215 DUNBARTON ROAD
DEXTER, ALABAMA

June 15, 1941

Mr. L. W. Hanks
Superintendent of Schools
Vistula, Washington

Dear Mr. Hanks:

At the suggestion of the Universal Teachers Agency I am writing to make application for the music position which is now open in your schools.

While the agency has already forwarded to you my record of qualifications and experience I am enclosing my own summary as well.

It is my understanding that this position includes the following work: (1) elementary school vocal supervision, (2) direction of a high school a cappella choir, and (3) the organizing and teaching of piano classes.

As you will see by the enclosed statement I have had six years of experience in both elementary and high school vocal work. I have given the names of a number of competent references who are well acquainted with my work.

I have spent the past two summers studying with two of the most competent instructors in class piano methods. In my work here in Dexter last year I had four small classes with a total of sixteen pupils. Now there are nearly double that number of applications for places in classes which will begin this fall. This seems to bespeak some success in a field which is new to me but in which I feel competent.

If Vistula were not so far from my home, I should be glad to make a personal application. If there is any further information which you wish to have concerning me, my training, or my experience I shall be glad to send it.

Very truly yours,

Lucy Hunter

Lucy is careful in the composition of her letter. She knows that Mr. Hanks will gain a general impression from the letter before he reads it for details. It so happens that Lucy studied typewriting in high school and has continued to use it with some skill ever since. But whether she writes a letter on the typewriter or in longhand she knows that it should look neat and attractive.

Lucy's statement of training and experience is very much like Jim McArthur's, which is found on page 176. She, too, has spent a little more money than was absolutely necessary on a good photograph. Since Lucy is rather good-looking and the picture does her justice, we believe Mr. Hanks will give it at least a couple of looks and perhaps read the letter and statement a little more carefully than he does some of the other letters which he receives.

Our prediction is that Lucy will get the job.

Chapter 3

THE SUPERVISOR MEETS A NEW COMMUNITY

Prologue

SAL-LY's-got-a-job, Sal-ly's-got-a-job, Sal-ly's-got-a-job, Sal-ly's-got-a-job . . ., so goes the rhythm of five of the six cylinders of Sally Howard's jallopy. Sally isn't worrying—much—about the absence of the sixth cylinder. If only this car will hang together until she can reach Metropolis, Indiana! Yesterday she nursed it carefully across three hundred miles of Missouri and Illinois highways while the thermometer flirted steadily with the one hundred mark. The reflection of the August sun on the concrete slabs shot white-hot arrows into her eyes all day.

Last night Sally stayed at a tourist camp—total charge, one dollar. That's a lot different from the way Sally travelled when she was in college and Pop paid the bills.

Only-a-hundred-miles-to-go, only-a-hundred-miles-to-go, only-a-hundred-miles-to-go. That's not the song of the motor. That's Sally's song of anticipation. She's got a job and she wants to get at it.

What's in the car besides Sally? First, a cello, of all things! Well, Sally is a good cellist and she hopes to be able to keep up her playing. (Flash!!! Picture of Miss Sally Howard stepping forth to play the Saint-Saëns Concerto before the assembled citizens of Metropolis. Much poise and confidence bolstered by the thought that the chartreuse gown, now packed in one of the cases on the running board, isn't bad at

28

all. Applause! Ovation!!) The three heavy looking boxes in the trunk compartment? In them may be found Sally's professional library of books and music. That long and slender package carefully placed on the front seat? Easy there! It contains four slender white batons with which Sally will bring forth the softest and loudest and quickest and slowest musical outpouring of the young scrapers, tooters, and yowlers of Metropolis. In those three travelling cases and two hat boxes is Sally's wardrobe. (It's got to do service for several years, now that she must pay for her own clothes.) Sally likes nice clothes and she'll always make a real effort to be well groomed. And, who knows but what there may be some rather attractive and eligible young men in Metropolis. Maybe . . .

Oh, well, it's all in a lifetime. Sally's on her way. She is a good musician. She is generally intelligent. She has shown marked aptitude as a teacher. She has enthusiasm and energy. She is conscientious and determined. She'll do a good job.

Only-a-hundred-miles-to-go . . . Sal-ly's-got-a-job . . . only-a-hundred-miles-to-go . . . Sal-ly's-got-a-job . . . only-a-hundred-miles . . . Sal-ly's-got . . . only-a-hundred . . . Sal-ly.

Metropolis! Get ready!

Good luck, Sally!

Reconnaissance

Today is August thirtieth. What's Sally Howard doing here in Metropolis so far ahead of time? School doesn't open until September sixth and Sally doesn't really have to be here until three o'clock on the afternoon of the fifth for the first teachers' meeting. She could easily have had a week more of vacation time.

Sally's a smart girl. She's going to know her community

before school starts. Her father is an important man in his own community and has been a member of the board of education for many years. She's heard him express some of his opinions of teachers and their ways—especially of those teachers who arrive in town at the last possible moment, race their cars to the high school building and breathlessly enter the first general teachers' meeting of the year with about thirty seconds to spare. Sally has always thought that teachers of that kind do not make very good impressions and records—and she's right.

A place to live. First, there is the problem of finding the right kind of living quarters. Mr. Huntington, the superintendent of schools in Metropolis, has a list of people who wish to provide room and board for teachers. He gives this list to Sally and makes some confidential suggestions concerning those places which he thinks would be best. Sally visits them and, because she is the first teacher to arrive for duty, she has first choice. So here she is, all settled at Mrs. Unger's home on Pine Street. Out come all the bags and boxes from her car. Her belongings are unpacked and put in place. Within twenty-four hours from the time of her arrival in Metropolis Sally is at home. Her room looks comfortable and Sally appears and acts as if she has settled down to an interesting job and a pleasant life ahead.

Music quarters and equipment. Now for the music room at the Metropolis High School. It's a little on the drab side but something can easily be done about that. A few color prints rightly placed, some furniture polish on the piano, and a few other deft touches will make a lot of difference. That looks like a pretty good piano but Sally has an idea as to how it is going to sound before she puts her hands on the keyboard. One chord is enough! It sounds worse than she thought. The

piano in the auditorium is just as bad. Who wants to lead
the singing in the first high school assembly or conduct a first
music class with handicaps like those pianos? They must be
tuned *before* school opens. No one would have bothered about
that unless Sally had reached here ahead of time.

What's in the music library? Now comes a careful checking over of stacks of octavo music, operettas, orchestra folios,
band books, and so on and on. They are all thoroughly mixed
up and it takes a lot of hard work to sort them into proper
piles and to classify them. Then comes the making of a list
so that Sally may easily refer to the resources of the library
which she has available.

On the shelves of the music storeroom are fifteen or twenty
instruments which belong to the schools. The cases are dusty
and it is easy to guess the condition of the instruments inside.
Sure enough, the clarinets need new pads and new corking;
the cello's bridge is cracked; all the brass instruments should
be cleaned and adjusted. So on down the line. Sally makes a
mental note that *next* year those instruments will be turned
over to an instrument repair man at the close of the school
year so that he can be working on them during the summer.
She knows that the work can be done that way at minimum
cost.

What materials are in use in the elementary schools? Exam-
ination of the records in Mr. Huntington's office shows what
music books have been ordered during recent years. Sally
has been fortunate in that her college methods course was
taught by a competent and alert instructor who believes that
young supervisors should be made acquainted with *all* principal materials on the market. To be on the safe side, she
quickly reviews the books and manuals that are in use in the
Metropolis schools.

A thorough search of the desk in the music room fails to disclose any trace of plans or outlines made by the preceding music supervisor. Sally's work would be much easier in the beginning if she had some way of knowing more about what was done last year. She resolves here and now to keep her plans, records, and materials in such shape that anyone who follows her will have the benefit of her experience and observation.

After two or three days of tedious and unpleasant work in examining and classifying grimy and dusty music, books, phonograph records, and instruments Sally finds herself with a good working knowledge of her equipment and supplies. She realizes that there are purchases to be made but she doesn't say anything about that just now—Mr. Huntington might feel that she is in too much of a hurry to spend money. But she has the facts on hand and in order; she will be able to make a successful appeal to Mr. Huntington at the proper time.

So much for the inside of the schools.

Some Journeys Downtown

Sally Howard knows that Mr. Huntington is her direct boss, but she also knows that she has a lot of bosses in town. The people she sees on the street—they are going to pay her salary. If they are the ones who have to dig down in their pockets for her monthly pay check, then they are the people for whom she is going to work. Her music program must be developed for them and their children.

Sally doesn't lump all the citizens of the community into a vague and meaningless group and think of them as "they." These people are *individuals*, each with his own likes and dislikes and interests. She wants them to feel a distinctly *per-*

sonal response to her work. If she can secure enough of this individual approval, the mass reaction of the community will be well founded and will take care of itself.

Every community has its own background of traditions and folkways. Sometimes they seem strange to the entering "foreigner." Awareness of and sensitivity to these living habits are necessary for Sally if she is to enter into community life in a truly thorough manner.

Who are these people? Where are they? What do they do? How will Sally come to know them and they to know her? How aggressive can she be in the matter of meeting and talking with them?

At this point Sally will need every bit of tact and ingenuity she can summon. The responsibility for meeting the community is definitely *hers*. She cannot let her opportunities for acquaintance with individuals depend upon a few school functions and the occasional visitor to her classroom. On the other hand, if she ventures forth into the town deliberately to make acquaintances and friends, she must avoid any appearance of being an ambitious busybody who is more concerned with political wire-pulling and personal promotion than with her work. However, it will be well for Sally to keep in the back of her mind a list of individuals and groups with whom she should have the best and most cordial of relationships. She will not be able to meet all of these within a short time and she cannot start out on an organized campaign to establish all these contacts immediately. Meeting the community will be an all-year job on which Sally will work quietly and tactfully, yet firmly. Let's take a look at the list.

1. *Board of education.* Sally met two members of the board of education when she made application in June. The

other three members, Dr. Wilson, Mrs. Henry and Mr. Thompson, were out of town or were unable to see her for some other reason. She should find some opportunity to meet them early in the school year. Perhaps they can best be approached through their children who are in school. Dr. Wilson plays viola in a string quartet composed of professional and business men in Metropolis. The quartet should be invited to play before an assembly or an appreciation class.

2. *Parent-Teacher officers and leaders.* Sally should learn the names of officers and leaders in PTA at an early date and should meet them as soon as the opportunity presents itself. If she is smart she will volunteer to help in the making of their programs but she will keep well in mind the fact that these people many times feel the responsibility of their positions and wish to assume most of the initiative and importance in the activities of their groups. She will be a follower here, not a leader.

3. *Individual citizens.* Every community has a group of influential and outstanding citizens—people who are not included in any of the general classifications of our list but who are important nevertheless. They may not have an official connection with the schools. They may not come into close contact with the music activities of the schools. They may not have children in school. But these business and professional people play an important part in the direction of community affairs. Sally cannot depend upon her professional channels to draw her into contact with them, and since she does not wish to appear to be a social-climber she will keep alert to all opportunities to become acquainted with them without going ahead too rapidly and thereby violating good taste. In managing these contacts it behooves Sally to proceed cautiously but not too timidly.

4. *Private music teachers.* Sally wants support from private music teachers—not complaints and competition. She must let them know that school music instruction will tend to increase the number of their pupils rather than to take them away. She must also make certain that they understand that she will not teach privately in competition with them. Members of good performance groups in the schools need specialized private instruction in addition to their school classes.

5. *Professional musicians and unions.* As soon as a good opportunity presents itself Sally will let it be known that her school organizations will not be used for public performances in such a manner that professional musicians will be deprived of income which is rightly theirs. This is a matter of school policy and she should immediately confer with her superintendent if any difficulties arise.

6. *Adult music organizations.* If there are any groups of adult music organizations in Metropolis they should have some contact with school music activities. They should feel that the schools are giving the kind of music training which will result in more and better-trained members for their groups in the future. Sally may find it possible to give some joint performances with some of these organizations.

7. *Newspapers and their staffs.* The two newspapers in Metropolis are good boosters for the schools. They are willing to give news space to school activities. If possible, Sally will find some member on the staff of each with whom she can work on all matters of publicity concerning music organizations and their doings. She must know the difference between news and nuisance. She must realize, too, that some of the advertising for events for which admission is charged should be paid advertising. Above all, she will avoid the appearance of trying to secure undue personal publicity.

8. *Service clubs.* The presidents and program chairmen of Rotary, Kiwanis, Lions, Exchange, etc., appreciate help from the school music department and are glad to have school organizations perform at their meetings. Sally will get across to them the following points: (1) her groups cannot appear until they have had an opportunity to get the year's work well under way; (2) they cannot appear too often during the year; and (3) the arrangements for such performances should be made well ahead of time.

9. *Church and related groups.* Sally may wish to establish definite affiliation with her own church group, but it will be well for her to know the pastors of all churches of all denominations and to be willing to assist them from time to time with their music problems. Is the high school choral training helping to provide the church with more and better singers? What about groups such as YMCA, YWCA, YMHA, YWHA? Are they doing anything with music?

10. *Near-by music educators.* Once in a while Sally should ask Mr. Huntington's permission to spend a day or a half-day observing the work of music supervisors in surrounding communities. If she does this she will be able to keep a fresher viewpoint and to benefit from the work and experience of others. In any event, she should know some of these other supervisors. She will need to talk with someone else who is trying to solve the same problems.

Getting to know the individuals and groups discussed above and gaining their support for the school music program of Metropolis is no small job. Sally is not going to rush it too much but she is going to keep its necessity clearly in mind at all times.

Sally is going to work for the people of the community of

Metropolis. She wants them to understand that she is at their service, yet she must never forget her professional standing and dignity. She must keep in touch with all affairs having to do with music in the community and at the same time not assume so many responsibilities that she will be unable to carry on her work effectively.

Many, many times Sally will look at teachers of other subjects and envy them. They don't have to provide groups for public performances in school and community nor do they have to devote much of their time to the development of adult community activities. Time and again Sally will wish to spend an evening at a movie or quietly at home, but there will be that choir rehearsal at which she promised to help, an operetta performance to supervise, a solo to play before a service club, or a special rehearsal with some pupils who are to enter a state contest. No rest for you this evening, Sally. You're not just teaching school; you're helping an entire community to have a grand time in its enjoyment of music.

Whose Schools?

These six school buildings in Metropolis—who owns them? The board of education? No. Mr. Huntington? No. The teachers? No. The citizens of the community own them.

For whom is the education in these buildings carried on? For the board of education, Mr. Huntington, or the teachers? Again, no. Again, the community.

Who is the eventual judge of the value and quality of the activities carried on in the name of education? Once more, the community.

Who is the real "boss" of the school system? The owners, the community.

Mr. Huntington has been superintendent of schools in Metropolis for twelve years. Not only has he grown more skillful during his years of administration, he has grown more tolerant. He knows that in a real democracy the people who own the institutions have the right to govern them. He knows that when that power is taken away from the people the democratic right of self-determination is lost.

During the past twelve years Mr. Huntington has known the people of this community to think and act in some strange ways. He has regretfully watched them sometimes elect the "wrong" kind of members to the board of education—members who seemed to have interests and ideas that were not advantageous to good education. Mr. Huntington has had to stand his ground against some of these members. But he has never given the impression that these schools are *his* schools; on the contrary, he has been working constantly to make the people of the community feel that these schools are *their* schools. It's a tough job sometimes.

Education in the Metropolis schools can go quietly on its way without interference or even apparent interest on the part of citizens for long periods of time. The community seems entirely willing that the administration and the teachers shall take over the school system and run it as they see fit. But—once in a while the taxpayers will assert themselves and strange things may happen. Mr. Huntington then spends some worried days and nights. His teachers become alarmed and even angry at the very idea of a lot of lay people, ignorant of educational methods, trying to tell them what they should do in the schools and how they should do it. The taxpayers sometimes wrathfully assert that these schools belong to *them* and that they are going to have some say in educational policies and procedures. Mr. Huntington, caught between his teachers and the citizens, wishes that the latter would act with a little more wisdom and deliberation, and at the same time that his teachers could get a little better understanding of the viewpoints and feelings of the citizens. The trouble generally lies in the fact that the teachers do not know the citizens and the citizens do not know the teachers.

Hard Times Knock at the Door!

Here's what may happen in Metropolis some day.

All the teachers in the Metropolis schools look worried this morning. As they enter the front door of the school building you can hear them asking one another questions: "Did you see the paper last night?" "Will we get a salary cut?" "Will some positions be abolished?" "Will the board of education stand back of us and our salaries?"

Yesterday evening the *Bugle-Courier* carried startling news. A group of citizens has demanded a decrease in the city budget and that implies a cut in the school budget, too. A hearing on the yearly budget is to be held in the high school auditorium on Friday night of next week. What will happen? Around that question will center much of the talk of Metropolis between now and the night of the meeting. Teachers will rail at the injustice and ignorance of cutting any costs of education. (Unfortunately most of their conversations will be among themselves because many of them aren't even acquainted with many taxpayers to whom they might talk with some influence.) Some of the taxpayers will become very indignant and maintain that it is high time that all this new and fancy stuff in education be cut out of the schools so that education can settle down to real fundamentals—with a consequent lowering of tax rates.

Mr. Huntington is greatly concerned. He has a double duty. He must represent the interests of the community and at the same time the interests of his teaching staff. But he has been through these sessions before. He is pretty sure that the worth of nearly all of his teachers can be proved with facts presented in open meeting. He feels that the community has confidence in the general policies and activities of the schools. However, he has some teachers who have not made much impression of any kind on the people of the community. What can he do to defend these teachers who are relatively unknown, both personally and professionally, to the people who pay their salaries? How much *can* and how much *should* he defend them? These are the questions which are making his life rather uncomfortable just now.

What about Sally? Is her work considered one of these "fads and frills" of modern education? What percentage of the people in Metropolis have been directly or indirectly affected by her music work? Has she become so valuable that her loss would be felt throughout the community? Or, if she were dismissed would nobody miss her or her work? What will happen when Old Man Watterson gets up in the budget meeting and contends that music is not needed in the schools; that no one ever spent a lot of money in giving *him* music lessons when *he* went to school; and that it would be best to save the money now being spent on music in the Metropolis?

The reactions of the audience will tell us what other people are thinking. Will we hear a lot of people asking the chairman of the meeting for recognition so that they can tell of the fine things that Sally's work has done for their families and their homes? Will they demand that music instruction appropriations be retained in the budget? Or will we see a lot of passive faces which seem to say "Sure, let's save money on music."

Sally isn't very much worried. Too many people have given her reassurance during the past ten days; too many people have called her on the telephone or stopped her on the street to tell her that *music cannot be dropped out of the schools.* Here are some samples of what people have said to her:

Mr. Horace Williams: "I'll resign as chairman of the Rotary Club program committee if anything happens to your job. We talked about it at yesterday's weekly meeting and everyone present said that your help to our club is the best assistance we have had in years."

Reverend Walton H. MacDougall: "I'm certain, Miss Howard, that all the members of our congregation are deeply appreciative of the things you have done for us and our choir. We feel that you are a community servant in the true sense of the word. I shall be at the meeting to speak for music in case anyone attacks it."

Miss Hattie Willoughby: "There was a time when I probably would have been glad to see music taken out of the schools because I felt that I was losing some of my music pupils as a result of it, but since you have been here my classes have been larger than ever because you are able to interest so many beginners through your class lessons. I'm doing everything I can around town to get people to say that they won't stand for music to be abolished from the schools."

Mr. Thomas Hartman (Tom): "Miss Howard, I've been head janitor at the High school building for sixteen years. You're the first music teacher we've ever had who has tried to make my work easier instead of harder. None of the rest of them would turn off the lights or lock the doors when they left after late practices. They wanted me to get the stage ready for them at five minutes' notice. You've been thoughtful of us fellows who take care of the building. We have a lot of relatives around town and they all vote. We're passing the word along to them to tell the right people not to stand for anything happening to your job."

Mrs. Sylvestre Tunnycliffe Worthington: "At the monthly meeting of the executive committee of the Metropolis Woman's Club we unanimously passed a resolution asking the city council and the board of education to refrain from taking any steps which would impair the development of the music instruction program in our schools. We feel that the contribution of your work to the cultural development of our community is one of the most valuable services provided by our schools."

Miss Willa Thornton: "Sally, those of us who have taught in the elementary schools for a long time have seen music supervisors come and go. You're the best one we have ever had. You really help us in our music teaching and you do it in a way that we like. The elementary teachers are going to put up a good scrap if anyone tries to cut out music."

Mrs. Martin Hays: "My son, Marty, has nearly always been in trouble in school, ever since he entered the first grade. I was afraid of what would happen to him in high school. The prospects didn't look good until he started his trombone lessons and got into the band. Now, thanks to your work, he's feeling much better toward the school and is coming along pretty well. I'm telling everyone that music is the most important thing in our schools."

Dr. Wilson: "Sally, perhaps I shouldn't talk outside of meeting but I want you to know that you have plenty of friends on the board of education. We all admire the work you've been doing. Don't worry."

Mr. Salvatore d'Amicio: "I haven't forgotten that you had your band in our Columbus Day parade last fall. I know that it was hard for you to do so soon after the beginning of school. I'm on the city council now."

Music's safe.

Sally's safe.

The reader's mental picture of Sally may be that of a clever, industrious and politically-minded young lady who depends upon personality, contacts and "pull" as the anchorage for her work and her position. Don't forget our earlier description of her: "She's a good musician. She is generally intelligent. She has shown marked aptitude as a teacher. She has enthusiasm and energy. She is conscientious and determined."

Chapter 4

STRUCTURE AND AUTHORITY OF THE SCHOOL SYSTEM

Who's Who?

IT is easy to make a diagram like this:

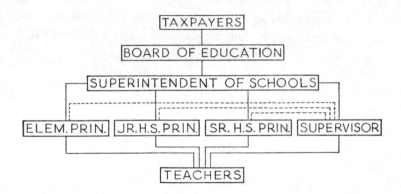

It is easy to understand this diagram. We can readily see how the authority of this school system is delegated. The board of education derives its authority from the taxpayers. The superintendent of schools is responsible to the board of education. The principals are responsible to the superintendent of schools, as is the supervisor. The dotted lines show responsibility of the principals and the supervisor to each other. The teachers are under the combined guidance of the principals and supervisor.

The words "taxpayers," "superintendent," "supervisor," etc., are names of *positions* in an impersonal diagram such as this one. As we look at the diagram we see only theoretical problems because *it hasn't any real people in it*. So long as we are concerned only with the *theory* of administrative and supervisory authority we shall remain remote from many of the most difficult daily situations which confront the music supervisor.

Here is another diagram:

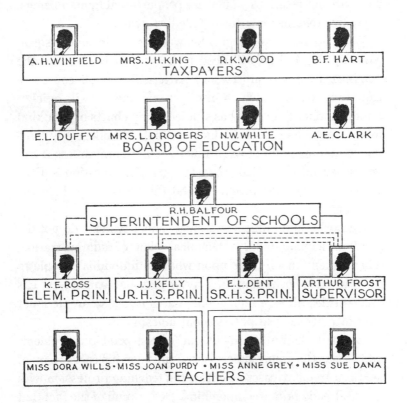

Now we have something different. Mr. Winfield, for instance, is not just any taxpayer—he is Mr. Winfield and he has his own personal characteristics and beliefs. Mrs. Rogers, who succeeded Mrs. King on the board of education this year, has views on education quite unlike Mrs. King's. Mrs. King has returned to the ranks of the taxpayer. Mr. Balfour as superintendent of schools is not at all like the superintendent in a school system ten miles away.

So it is with all the people represented in this diagram. They are not positions. They are people—real human beings. They live together in a town called Millvale.

When Arthur Frost begins his work as music supervisor in Millvale this fall he will need to know how he fits into the administrative and supervisory pattern there. Of course he can study a chart such as our first one and he will quickly understand it because he has studied many charts of that kind in the education courses which he took in college. But his understanding will not be of much value to him unless it can go far beyond a knowledge of positions. The question is, How well will he be able to understand the people who hold the positions?

Authority and influence in most school systems do not depend principally upon a technical plan of administration. They depend much more upon what an individual is able to build into his position in the way of personal leadership. His official title will be a hollow one unless it has an ample inner core of personal and professional investment.

Let us talk frankly about one of the principal problems which face the young supervisor of music in his early years of service. In many cases he enters the teaching profession with a title already bestowed upon him. He is proud of the fact that he can place on his stationery "Supervisor of Music." It looks well and it sounds well to a young fellow who is just getting started. But it should not look or sound too well for his own good.

This position in Millvale is Arthur's first one. He is just out of college. Easy now, Arthur. Don't let that bright and shiny new title get the best of you. Don't become intrigued with the idea that you are a high-ranking supervisory officer right off. The tendency to do that very thing has probably resulted in more grief to beginning music supervisors than have all other causes combined.

Some school administrators doubt the wisdom of allowing the title of "supervisor" to be used by anyone who does not have to his credit several years of successful teaching.

Arthur, there is a way to capitalize upon your inexperience. It is a way which will stand you in good stead with many people, and you will learn a lot at the same time. Remember that all of us feel somewhat magnanimous when we are helping someone else. We feel more self-important when giving help than when receiving it. We are flattered when someone asks us for help. So if you are really smart you will make a lot of people feel that they are responsible for making you into a good music supervisor.

When you go to the first teachers' meeting take a look at the lady sitting on the far end of the second row of seats. That's Miss Flora Green. She has sat in that same seat at every teachers' meeting in Millvale for sixteen years. When you begin your rounds you will find her in the fourth-grade room where sixteen groups of children have been taught by her in as many years. She has seen a number of music supervisors come and go in that time. To her, at this point, you are just another in the line of succession. And, to be truthful about the matter, she has not thought very highly of some of your predecessors. So far as she is concerned most of them have been lacking in ability as teachers and have taken an unjustifiably superior attitude in their supervision.

Miss Green is a really good teacher. She is somewhat on the formal side of methods in general and the discipline in her room is more strict than that which may be found in most rooms, but she is the kind of teacher who always has some definite goals in mind—and she generally reaches them. She is serious about this matter of teaching. The pupils who have been in her classes look back upon their year under her guidance as a time during which they really learned something. She has kept up with the times. No teacher in Millvale is better read or more alert concerning current educational theory and practice.

Miss Green is now looking in your direction, Arthur. What is she saying to herself? Do you suppose she could be saying, "So, we've got a new music supervisor!" (You should hear the way she says that word "supervisor" to herself! It wouldn't make you feel good.) "And that's the green young fellow who is going to tell me how to teach? Humph!"

It is true that Miss Green doesn't know as much about music as you do but she does know teaching from the ground up. And now it's up to you to supervise her. Of course you can go into her room and spout a lot of music facts and technicalities. You can show off your musicianship and feel rather proud of it. But when it comes to *teaching* you had better watch your step because you are going to be showing off your initial efforts (other than in practice teaching) before an old-timer to whom teaching is both an art and a profession.

Many, many times Miss Green has watched your predecessors struggle with her classes and has despaired of their feeble efforts in class management, organization, and procedures in general. She would have felt greatly complimented if any of them had ever sought her advice and counsel about teaching problems. But no, they would not have thought of doing such a thing. They were "supervisors" and therefore somewhat above the teachers.

Now, Arthur, take your cue from this situation. Do everything you can to make Miss Green feel that she is helping you to become a good teacher. She can do it too. There's no need to be afraid of her. She is a little stern on the surface but you'll be surprised how quickly she will soften when you say or imply to her that you have heard that she is one of the very finest teachers in the system and that you hope you can learn something about teaching from her. Make a quiet little deal with her in which you agree to supply the musical skill if she will do her part on the pedagogical side.

What will happen? In the first place, you will have splendid results with the pupils because you and Miss Green will be doing real co-operative teaching. After all, isn't that the prime requisite of good supervision? In the second place, you will be learning about teaching from a master craftsman. Thirdly, Miss Green will be more enthusiastic about her music work than ever before. Finally, Miss Green will be a strong supporter of yours. Why shouldn't she tell people that you are the best music supervisor she's ever seen when she privately thinks, and with some justice, that she is responsible for your success?

Let us leave further discussion of your relation to classroom teachers until later. Just now we shall examine our diagram of the Millvale schools, beginning at the top with the taxpayers. What are your responsibilities to all these people represented here?

The Taxpayers

In the preceding chapter we have seen how Sally Howard went about the business of meeting the people of the community of Metropolis. In general, Arthur, your approach to the people of Millvale will involve many similar situations and problems. Of course Millvale does not have the same groups and organizations. The social and economic backgrounds of Millvale life may be vastly different from those in Metropolis. The traditions and history of the two towns may be very unlike. But the fact remains that you will find it necessary to investigate carefully and tactfully the resources and forces of the community in which you will work and to chart your course of approach and action upon the fundamental concept that you have come here to work for the taxpayers of Millvale in the job of making music a more vital force in their lives.

From a purely technical standpoint these taxpayers have no direct control over you and your work. They cannot hire or fire you. That power is delegated by them to the board of education, otherwise there would be great confusion in the administration of the schools. Neither can these taxpayers take direct charge of the police force, the street department, the fire department or any of the other activities which are under communal control. But, in the end, the taxpayers and citizens are the real owners and bosses in the community. That is democracy in action. Sometimes the employees of these community agencies become capricious toward the background of authority of the citizens. This is dangerous. Citizens have a way of remembering those people who violate the traditions, the feelings, the beliefs, and the authority of the community group.

The Board of Education

These are the people with whom you have entered into contract. They are the elected or appointed representatives of the community of Millvale. Sometimes they are called the "school board" or the "school directors." They are "directors" in the same sense that a corporation has a board of directors to represent the stockholders and to assume the responsibility for control.

Since Millvale is a medium-sized community your relations with the board of education will be moderately close. Were you in a small community you might find yourself under much more direct supervision by the board members because community control in smaller towns is naturally more intimate. If you were in a large city it is likely that you would have little direct contact with board members. In these large units the relation between "employer" and "employee" is more impersonal. The choice and administration of personnel is left more completely to the appointed officers of administration.

There are very few localities where the supervisor of music does not have some relatively direct dealings with the board of education. Because music plays a more active part in community affairs, because it involves situations which require some formulation of public policy, and because music equipment many times requires unusual expenditures, the music supervisor usually has more direct dealings with the board of education than have teachers of such subjects as history and mathematics.

Arthur, there is one very important point to remember about your relation to the board of education. *You should never deal directly with the board or any of its individual members without having explicit directions from your super-*

intendent of schools to do so. This does not mean that you should have no contact with board members. In the course of normal life in the community there will be many times when you will visit with them as you will with other people. You will have opportunity to discuss your work with them from an educational standpoint. But never raise any matters of official business (salary, supplies, school routines, etc.) with them unless your superintendent directs you to do so. You should initiate all official business through your superintendent.

It would be difficult to estimate the number of young music supervisors who have had severe set-backs at the beginning of their careers as a result of disregard for official etiquette. No school administrator approves of staff members under his direction going "over his head" to the board of education on matters which should be cleared through him. There may be times when you will have problems which your superintendent feels should be settled by the board and he may ask you to talk to members and lay your story before them. In turn, they will know that the superintendent has provided clearance and they will consider such a move ethical. However, board members themselves are inclined to be suspicious of people who skirt the usual channels of authority.

The Superintendent of Schools

This is the man, Arthur, who has been hired to administer the affairs of the schools in the name of the board of education. He is a man whose professional training has made him into a specialist in the business of school management. He has the principal responsibility for formulation of the educational policies of the schools. The board generally follows his recommendations in those matters because they have employed him so that they may have the advantage of his skill and professional advice. In some instances the superintendent may also have supervision of matters financial as well as educational. That depends upon the size of the community and the kind of organization in effect.

This is the man to whom you will be directly responsible. He is your official "contact" man with the board and the community.

Superintendents vary in personality just as greatly as do other people. One of them may be very strict and hold you strictly accountable for all your time and work. Another may be the kind of fellow who will let you alone to work out your own program and responsibility.

You see, Arthur, it isn't possible for you to predict any hard and fast relations to the superintendent. All the books on educational administration cannot give you all the guidance you will need in your relations with Mr. Balfour, the superintendent in Millvale. It is up to *you* to study Mr. Balfour. Remember what we have said before, Mr. Balfour is a person, not a position. You will have to find out how Mr. Balfour wants you to work, and then do it that way. Certainly you may help him change his mind sometimes but you will do it in such a way that he will want to agree with you about the changes—not merely because you are argumentative with him.

Nearly all superintendents of schools have been teachers and many of them have also had experience as principals. They generally achieve their positions as superintendents because they have been aware of and are sensitive to school problems. Any intelligent superintendent knows that one of the best signs of a good administration is a loyal supporting staff of principals, supervisors, and teachers.

Mr. Balfour will be grateful to you if you will do everything possible to keep your relations with him pleasant and effective. He will consider you efficient if you keep him well posted with regard to what is going on in your department so that he may never seem to be poorly informed. He will appreciate your deference to his authority in those instances in which he finds it necessary to take a stand on some issue. Yet he will wish to have you present your contentions clearly, forcefully, and pleasantly. He will be grateful to you for your loyalty to his administration.

Unless Mr. Balfour is very different from most superintendents he likes to feel that the teachers under his direction are constantly growing in professional stature. He is pleased when he can promote people in his own system. He is even more pleased sometimes when other towns elect his staff members to more important posts. If he sees that you are developing into a much better music supervisor while you are "his" supervisor he will look upon you as one of his personal products and will always be glad to support you.

Don't be afraid to tell Mr. Balfour once in a while (but not too often or too pointedly) that you are grateful for his guidance and advice. He likes kind words the same as anyone else.

Principals

Here, Arthur, we come to one of the more delicate and at the same time intricate problems of school administration and supervision. What is the exact relation of the building principal and the supervisor? The wrong conception of this relation has caused many music supervisors some of the unhappiest times of their lives.

Let's look at the principal's side of the picture first. He is charged with both administrative and educational control of all the pupils in his building. Under the heading of "administration" come his duties relating to attendance, charge of the physical properties of building and grounds, conferences with parents, discipline, and so on. At the same time his "educational" functions require him to stand responsible for the teaching and learning which go on in his building. If he is a really good principal he will see to it that the teaching efforts of his building staff and those of the visiting "special" teachers are blended into a stream of activities which will assure true learning on the part of the pupils. It is true that some principals spend most of their time and effort on matters "administrative" rather than "educational," in which situations you or any other teacher or supervisor may take matters pretty much in your own hands and do as you please. But in such cases it is safe to predict that the work accomplished in those buildings will not be of high calibre.

The skilled and efficient principal is a true "integrator" of all activities in his building. Who else is in position to see to it that the many separate channels of experience which pupils encounter finally merge into a meaningful whole? This general supervision is clearly the duty of the principal.

On the other hand, along comes the music supervisor with a city-wide plan for the development of music education. He has a course of study. He wishes to achieve some unity of standards of music work throughout the school system. Perhaps he also wishes to establish uniformity of methods and classroom procedures. He has been employed to supervise music instruction and he wants an opportunity and a clear road to carry out his ideas and plans.

Now do you see the problem? Which of these two people is to have the real power of making the decision regarding the

direction and form which music education shall take? Shall
the principal have that power and insist upon what he believes
to be the needs of his particular building? Or shall the supervisor have the right to carry out a system-wide plan based
upon his specialized training and experience in music?

These questions have been the cause of innumerable
"battles" between principals and supervisors. Whenever co-
operation between principal and supervisor has *not* been
achieved *the pupils themselves have been the losers*. In many
such instances the music program has come almost to a dead
halt.

In your education courses at Northern Teachers College
you read several books having to do with school administration and supervision. You probably found that they did not
agree on the boundaries of authority of principals and supervisors. Some of them almost evaded definite statements on
such matters. No wonder! Each school system makes its
own patterns and generally these patterns are developed
partly upon a basis of the personalities involved as well as
upon educational subjects. And no one can predict the out-
come of mixing personalities.

All of which is by way of saying, Arthur, that the real scope
of your supervisory authority will depend greatly upon the
extent to which you can effect good working relations with
your principals. Remember that a principal is the direct
"boss" of a school building. He lives and works there day
after day. The first responsibility of the teachers is to him.
The special teacher or supervisor who visits the building occasionally will be severely handicapped unless he has the en-
dorsement and support of the principal.

There have been instances of supervisors who have made
an issue of whether they or the principals were to direct the

music education program. Sometimes the supervisors have won out and have had their lines of authority definitely established by the superintendent or the board of education. They have been given authority to go ahead with their own plans and the principals have been instructed to leave the music work entirely in the hands of the music supervisors. Such victories are indeed empty ones for the supervisors. The principals then wash their hands of the whole music business, and you can rest assured that teachers will generally give their first loyalties to their principals unless conditions are exceptional.

This business of effecting a proper working agreement with principals is sometimes difficult. Some principals are generally suspicious of supervisors of any kind, especially young ones who are not yet thoroughly established in classroom procedures. Others are just not interested in the development of the music program. Whenever you find either of these types it is part of your job to start "selling" your program and your work. You will not win your point by trying to impress them with your "authority" as a supervisor.

It is not in the province of this book to discuss the relative values of "musical" approaches and "integrated" approaches. However, some mention of them is necessary because of administrative implications. On one hand we may have a truly "musical" course of study and program of instruction which emanates from the supervisor and which seeks to establish system-wide standards and procedures in music, apart from relation and integration with other subjects. On the other hand there is the possible genesis of music activities and learning from other parts of the curriculum, such as social studies. The principal is many times likely to see advantages in the latter procedure because he may regard music as something to complete and intensify the general learning activities which are going on in his school.

What are you going to do, Arthur, when the principal of the Bryant School asks you to teach a group of South American songs to the fifth grade for a forthcoming pageant just at the time you find that the class is ready to start upon certain steps for technical musical development? **Are** you going to hold out for your musical and technical accomplishments or will you drop them for the time being and teach the songs for the pageant? Questions of this kind will be constant and troublesome companions for you in today's schools. How to answer them? We don't know. Strong argument can be advanced for both sides of the case. It is up to you to use your best judgment.

We can safely advise you, we believe, concerning one point. The closer your relation and understanding with the principal the easier is the solution of such problems. Solutions are difficult when you and the principal are on opposite sides of the fence. Are you responsible or is the principal responsible for establishing this better understanding? Theoretically, the answer would be 50–50. Actually, we're of the opinion that the greater part of the effort must come from you. The principal is on his "home ground" when you come into his building. You're a "foreigner." We believe that you will find it advantageous to follow his ideas more than your own—at least in the beginning and until you are in a position to try to win him over to your way of thinking. You will find yourself in this position when the principal begins to feel that you come to his building to be of real help to him, his teachers, and the pupils rather than for the primary purpose of developing a music program that is only to your own liking.

This doesn't mean, Arthur, that you should sacrifice **your** ideas and ideals of good music education and that you should content yourself with being a mere itinerant music teacher who does odd jobs for all parts of the curriculum other than music itself. You *must* hold to the furtherance of music as an *art*. We believe that you will accomplish your aim by *beginning* at the place where you will receive the greatest support from principals, teachers, and pupils. After you have made the right kind of start and have gained momentum you will find it relatively easy to develop a blended program which will be acceptable to everyone concerned.

If you are not able to obtain support from the beginning and to keep it, you will have a long, hard road ahead of you. We are spending a lot of time here talking to you about principals because they are important people. They really represent your point of contact with the general curriculum. More than that, they are the people who control most of the activities and attitudes of the classroom teachers. If a principal indicates to his teachers that he wants something done in music, then it is likely that it will be done. If the teachers think that you and the principal are at odds on the music program you are going to have a hard time of it.

Above all, do not feel fortunate if you find a principal who is willing to let you alone and pay no attention to what is happening in music. Too many young supervisors accept this kind of situation as approval and support. Far from it. It merely means that the principal is not sufficiently interested in what you are doing to pay any attention to it. A disinterested principal is a distinct liability. A contentious principal who has some ideas of his own on music, even though they are not in agreement with yours, is much more likely to become a strong supporter.

Do not fail to call at the principal's office the first thing when you visit a school. Regulations in force in most school systems consider the supervisor under the jurisdiction of a principal, just as are teachers, when he is in that principal's building. The principal is the chief officer of instruction. Call at his office again upon leaving the school. Have at least a brief visit with him. Make certain that he knows what work you are doing and how your plans are coming along. Some very successful supervisors find it best to write all instructions to teachers in triplicate—one copy going to the teacher, one to the principal, and one to the supervisor's file.

Do not wait for the principal to ask you for reports of progress. Give them to him without his asking. He may not show much interest in them at first, and if such is the case it then becomes your job to make him show interest.

The Teachers

You will recall, Arthur, that earlier in this chapter we spoke of Miss Flora Green. She is only one of the teachers in Millvale. There is not another teacher in the system of whom you could say "She's just like Miss Green." The approach to supervision of classroom teachers cannot be undertaken with the feeling that all teachers are alike and that they all respond to the same kind of treatment.

Many books have been written on supervision and its functional aspects. We could quote to you several well-considered and highly polished statements and definitions of supervision, but most of them would be particularly applicable to a large city school system with its maze of administrative and supervisory officers. We are thinking here of Millvale and thousands of similar communities. Incidentally, we believe that supervision in some of the larger cities would be better if it were considered in the light of human values rather than in the cold and hard manner with which it is sometimes regarded.

Coming down to the simplest statement of the functions of supervision, isn't it true that a good supervisor is one who gives the greatest amount of help and encouragement to the classroom teacher to the end that she may constantly and consistently grow in her power to teach music better in the period between the visits of the supervisor?

It is important to note here that we are not talking of the special music teacher who assumes all the responsibility for music instruction as is sometimes done in departmentalized schools. We are considering the problems of the supervisor who makes a periodic visit to each classroom—classrooms in which the regular teacher carries on the greater part of the work.

For our part, we should like to substitute some title such as "Co-operating Music Teacher" or "Helping Music Teacher" for "Supervisor" in many instances. Teachers like to think of specialists as coming to help them rather than merely to inspect them. A young music supervisor could many times make a strongly favorable impression upon a classroom teacher if he would say, "I'm not here to supervise. I'm here to *help*. You are a good teacher in many subjects. I'm a specialist in music. The two of us should be able to get together and do a good job."

There are two extremes of procedure which are many times followed. Both are eventually unsuccessful. The first one is immediately suicidal in most instances.

First, the new supervisor comes in briskly and efficiently and asks the classroom teacher to proceed with the music lesson. He sits down, assumes a judicial air, and evaluates the lesson. After the lesson is finished he may spend a few minutes airing his musical learning to teacher and class. Then after a few crisp instructions to the teacher regarding work to follow he leaves with the feeling that he certainly has impressed everyone with his knowledge and importance.

Second, there is the supervisor who comes into the room and merely teaches a lesson, leaving the classroom teacher out of the activity entirely. The lesson may or may not have some bearing on work previously done or work which will follow. This kind of a supervisor is really a "guest artist" and is making no real contribution to the continuity of the music program in that room or to the further development of the teaching skill of the classroom teacher.

Between these two extremes is the ground of co-operative teaching. Here the work is shared by teacher and supervisor. The teacher and pupils look upon the supervisor as a person with special talents and skill who comes to help them through the more difficult phases of their music learning. There is a feeling of joint responsibility for the progress of the class. The supervisor and the teacher work side by side without concern regarding authority.

The guidance and planning of work should not be solely in the hands of the music supervisor. Courses of study, outlines, and plans should contain many suggestions which have originated with classroom teachers. These teachers should feel that their own efforts are valuable contributions to the general structure and content of the music curriculum. Do not be afraid to give ample credit to teachers for their contributions.

Plans and outlines should be simple and direct. They should be prepared in such a way that teachers will feel that they are helpful instead of time-wasting and burdensome. Complicated and poorly arranged outlines which are hard to read and understand are distinct liabilities.

If you find it advisable and possible to hold teachers'
meetings devoted to music, make certain that your program
for such meetings is well planned and executed. Teachers
become very weary of meetings at which someone simply gets
up and talks on and on without any apparent purpose or organization. Start the meetings on time, keep them brief and
snappy, and see that they end promptly.

We cannot emphasize too much the necessity for the supervisor's visit to be a friendly one. The hard, brittle visit that
is lacking in personal warmth accomplishes little.

If you are a good musician, the teachers and their pupils
will find it out without your having to emphasize the point
yourself. Their first interest in you will be a personal and
human one. As they come to know you and to like you better
they will accumulate a knowledge of and a respect for your
talent and skill.

One of the most successful music supervisors in the country
has always belittled his musical superiority to his teachers.
When he accomplishes something good he virtually says to
them "See there! I'm not much of a musician but I got that
done. *You* can do it too." What a contrast that is to the supervisor who is constantly emphasizing his own skill in such
a way that the average classroom teacher despairs of accomplishing anything because of her more limited musical en-
dowment.

Encouragement of the classroom teacher is of first importance and in the long run this method pays the music
supervisor larger dividends than does high-pressure selling
of himself.

Remember, Arthur, that the classroom teacher works in
many subject-matter fields while you deal in only one. What
do you know about the content and techniques of courses in

language arts, social sciences, science, mathematics, graphic and plastic arts, health and safety, physical education, and so on down the line? The classroom teacher is supposed to be well grounded in all these fields. Is it any wonder that she sometimes falls short in your *one* subject of music?

By the way, it is a very good idea for the music supervisor to observe and study the teaching of some of these other subjects from time to time. It is an excellent way to learn to be a good *teacher*—regardless of the subject matter involved. If you will watch a good classroom teacher work through the entire curriculum for a day you will learn a lot about the fundamentals of good teaching. It will also help you to see how music may be better fitted into the daily educational activities of pupils.

Your occasional visit to a classroom certainly cannot be regarded as the main stem of a good music education program. Without the day-by-day work of the classroom teacher you cannot accomplish the most satisfactory results. True, you may give interesting lessons from time to time and they may be enjoyed, but the rate of growth of the class will be very slow.

So, then, your real job in supervision is centered around in-service music training of classroom teachers. Do not stop to rant at the scanty preparation which these teachers have received in their training schools. That will not do one bit of good. They had to study many things while you were busy majoring in music. Do not waste any time complaining about things which you think are wrong. Just start working alongside these teachers and help them develop into better music teachers. They are already skilled in teaching. You give them assistance on the music side and all of you will benefit.

The Supervisor

The in-school functions of the music supervisor may be summarized as follows: (1) general planning and co-ordination of the music program from kindergarten through high school; (2) furnishing of expert musical knowledge and skill for the entire program; (3) active teaching of special music groups; (4) co-operative teaching with classroom teachers; and (5) in-service training of classroom teachers.

Now for a word of warning. In recent years the truly supervisory functions of the music supervisor have generally been decreasing rather than increasing. This is a trend which should be carefully noted and studied by the profession. The music "supervisor" is coming more and more to be a "special teacher" who does active teaching of special music groups and who remains "on call" for help and consultation in regular classroom work. Thus do we see the music supervisor achieving direct contact with fewer and fewer pupils, sometimes only with those of higher abilities who are in special organizations. Is this a trend which is "just happening" or are there reasons for it? We believe that there are several reasons.

A position that is truly supervisory must have the support of administrators, principals, and teachers. What has been the attitude of many of these people toward the music supervisor? In many instances it has been one of indifference.

What have they wanted and expected from a music supervisor? Human values of the kind that make pupils and teachers welcome the supervisor's visit; superior and authoritative musicianship; superior teaching ability and skill in classroom techniques; a thorough understanding of the relation of music to the entire curriculum; and willingness for complete co-operation.

Certainly that is a large order, but it must be filled if the true status of supervisor is to be achieved. Why should the classroom teacher be "supervised" unless the "supervisor" is really superior?

The music supervisor who wanders aimlessly from room to room, just teaching a class here and there; the music supervisor who pays no attention to trends and development of the entire curriculum; the music supervisor who is less skilled than most of the classroom teachers in the business of classroom procedures; the music supervisor who is incapable of in-service music training of classroom teachers; the music supervisor who is deficient in musical talent and training— none of these will have sufficient support in his claim to a real supervisory status.

So much for what other people sometimes think about music supervision. What about the music supervisors themselves? Too many times they are willing to see the influence of their positions decrease because of a corresponding decrease in the responsibility and hard work involved. The business of being a *supervisor* is hard work. It is much harder work than is direct teaching of special and limited groups. The supervisor has a never-ending program of work. The special teacher may many times consider his work finished when he has completed the required number of teaching periods.

Is real leadership a part of the supervisor's job? It should be. The music curriculum has been expanding rapidly. To-day it includes many activities which have been introduced only in recent years. The greatest personnel need at this time is not for specialists who can handle parts of the music program but rather for supervisors of high calibre who can build and direct the entire program.

Chapter 5

PLANS AND SCHEDULES

THE Middletown board of education met last week and the most important problem of the session was the reduction of next year's school budget. During the discussion one of the board members questioned the value of the work being done by the music supervisor, Miss Ethel Williams. The discussion, in part:

Board Member: "Do we really need a music supervisor? Can't we let the grade teachers handle their own music? The manual training man in the high school used to play in a band. He can take over the band rehearsals. One of the English teachers used to sing in a college glee club. She can handle the chorus work. I don't see why we need a full-time music teacher running around the school system. There's probably not enough work to keep her busy all the time."

Superintendent: "Miss Williams is a good music supervisor. She has been well trained. She is very conscientious in her work and always seems to be busy. I don't happen to have a written schedule of her daily or weekly activities but I'm certain she doesn't waste any time. She goes to the elementary schools several times a week, I don't know just how many. She has some band and chorus rehearsals and also gives some class and private lessons."

Suppose the reply of the superintendent could have been:

Superintendent: "Gentlemen, I have here a written summary of every week of Miss Williams' work since she first came here. Let's take a look at last week's schedule to get an idea of what she does. Miss Williams visited thirty elementary rooms and spent twenty minutes in each one, teaching and supervising. She had three twenty-minute after-school meetings with various elementary classroom teachers who needed special help. During the week she held six band, orchestra, and chorus rehearsals with a total of 240 students. Here's her record of twelve twenty-minute periods of class instruction for 52 instrumental students, also a record of ten private periods of instrumental instruction for advanced students.

"On Friday, Miss Williams directed a special music assembly in the high school and that required two extra rehearsal periods. Oh, yes, here's her note of an operetta rehearsal in one of the elementary schools after school on Tuesday and I see that on Wednesday she took the boys' glee club to sing before the Rotary Club during the noon hour. And, gentlemen, Miss Williams has what no other teacher in our school can claim—a Saturday schedule during which she gives additional private and class instruction. Then on Sunday, though she doesn't include it in this schedule, I know that she helps several of the church choirs in our community.

"Miss Williams is one of the most efficient and businesslike teachers in our system. Her work is carefully organized. She provides me with a schedule of this kind so that I know just what she is doing all the time. She says that she wants a well-balanced, well-organized program and that the making of this weekly schedule gives her a fine opportunity to see, on paper, just what she is doing.

"My own opinion is that Miss Williams is one of our most valuable teachers. I know that you do not have opportunity to see her at work, but here is a file of her weekly schedules and I think that if you will examine them, all of you will be greatly impressed by the way in which she organizes her time and efforts to give us good music in our schools and our community."

It is not difficult to imagine the difference of the effect on the members of the board of education if the superintendent were to make the second reply instead of the first. Let's remember that the average board of education member is a business or professional man who admires and respects order and purpose in planning. Too many times those whose work has to do with music have had applied to them such descriptions as "temperamental," "impractical," "unbusinesslike," and "inefficient."

Music instructors must necessarily spend a substantial part of their time on activities which are sometimes included under the "extra-curricular" classification. This situation demands the formation of daily and weekly schedules far different from those of science, English, or mathematics instructors who meet the same groups of pupils at the same hours on every day of the week. Because of the flexibility of the music instructor's schedule there is always present the temptation to let that schedule become flabby, unorganized, and even chaotic. This is most dangerous to the quality of the work which the instructor produces. It is also dangerous to the reputation of the instructor. Unless he can make his schedule appear businesslike and efficient he will lose the respect of pupils, other instructors, and administrators and will lay himself open to criticism by his community and the board of education.

Some administrators will not *demand* a daily or weekly schedule from a music supervisor and some may not even request it. However, if the music supervisor must be located immediately or something be known about the schedule of his work, the administrator is placed in an embarrassing position unless that information is on his desk or in his files. Lack of knowledge of the work of these "roving" teachers makes the administrator appear inefficient, and he will blame the supervisor for not keeping him informed.

Music supervisors, particularly those who are relatively inexperienced, should take the initiative in providing schedules and plans rather than wait for some administrative officer to request them. It must be remembered that there are inefficient and unbusinesslike administrators too. They are the ones who do not have much influence with the board of education or in the community, and who are most liable to dismissal. Therefore, there is all the greater reason why a supervisor must establish and protect himself by providing proof of his efficiency in written form so that it may be filed for inspection by anyone.

Conferences with Administrators

It is well for the supervisor to sit down with his administrative superior with some regularity and talk over general and specific long-range problems of the music program. What is the eventual instrumentation toward which he is working in his bands and orchestras? How many and which of the elementary classroom teachers are showing increase in skill and responsibility in the handling of the daily music period? What has caused the falling-off of membership in the boys' glee club? Can more students be sent to state and regional festivals and competitions? Are the church choirs of the community benefitting from the choral training program in the high school? Are the service clubs demanding too many appearances of his performing organizations, or should there be more such appearances? What will be the budget requirements of the music department for next year? Is the time ripe for the introduction of class piano instruction?

Hundreds of questions such as these are the ever-present problems of the music supervisor. They should not be "sprung" on an administrator for quick decision and opinion in a hurried five-minute conference. Such questions should be under constant and thoughtful consideration, and discussion concerning them should take place far ahead of the time for their eventual solution. There must be continued "selling" of these problems to the administrator so that he will come to think of them as being a part of *his* responsibility rather than as troublesome problems which the supervisor throws at him with no preparation and background.

Many supervisors never go near the administrative office unless they are sent for or unless they want something. This should not be. The supervisor should confer with the administration regularly concerning the more important aspects of his work. When he goes to such conferences he should take with him a written memorandum of the points which he wishes to discuss and this memorandum should be left with the administrator. The average superintendent has many affairs of many kinds under his supervision. It is a compliment and a courtesy to him if a supervisor who is conferring with him gives evidence of having carefully thought out what he wishes to accomplish in the conference. The superintendent is then likely to find time and inclination for discussion whenever the supervisor asks for it.

One supervisor has made a wise move in providing his superintendent with a loose-leaf notebook for the filing of all matters pertaining to music. His weekly schedules, his memorandum notes of current problems, his reports of all kinds, his budget estimates, etc., are all prepared on paper which will fit into this notebook. When he goes to the superintendent's office he takes this notebook from a shelf there and places in it the material which he has come to discuss. His record and the history of his work are in that book. It is available to anyone who wishes to see it. Incidentally, that superintendent regards his music supervisor as one of the most competent persons in the entire school system, and the supervisor thinks that his notebook is the best job insurance he has.

Reports

The supervisor mentioned in the preceding paragraph never fails to file monthly and yearly reports.

At the end of each month he reviews his weekly schedules and makes a summary of his work for that month. This summary includes such items as: the number of elementary classrooms visited, conferences with classroom teachers, classes regularly taught, rehearsals of organizations, private lessons, public performances, special assemblies, attendance at professional meetings, etc. Significant trends and events in his music education program are noted briefly. Special developments are treated more elaborately. The preparation of his monthly report requires only an hour or so of work. It is well worth the effort.

At the end of the year this supervisor takes all his monthly reports and makes a grand summary from them. Then he spends some time and thought in writing a history of the year's work. What has been accomplished? What difficulties have been met, and how? What are the problems ahead for next year's work? What recommendations has he to make?

In other words, this supervisor reports to his board of directors in the same manner as does an intelligent and efficient officer of a corporation. The administrative officers and board of education members respect and appreciate his businesslike attitude in keeping them informed of his work.

The Course of Study

In this volume there is no attempt to consider the content or procedures of the music curriculum. In viewing the need for a course of study we are thinking of it in terms of its value as a "statement of policy" of the music educator and his fellow workers.

A decade ago a wave of course of study making swept the country. Its crest soon passed and many of its products have long been forgotten. The weakness inherent in most of them lay in the fact that they were built purely as academic structures, after which everyone forgot all about them.

Every music supervisor should have a course of study. He should have in written form, for general distribution throughout the school system and to residents of the community, a general statement of the purposes and standards of his music program. This general statement should be accompanied by a more specific treatment of individual problems with at least a brief suggestion of procedures to be followed.

Now the most important thing is to keep this course of study in a constant state of revision. It should never be looked upon as a finished or static piece of work. It should always be fresh and timely. Last year's weaknesses will be strengthened this year. Teachers will look upon it as an up-to-date guide for their work rather than as an old, time-worn object that has been on their desks for years.

Then when someone wants to know something of the music department and its work the supervisor can hand over a copy of this year's course of study and the whole story will be right there.

Courses of study are too often looked upon as principally outlines of methods. Certainly some methods should be included in a good course of study. But there is a more important function of which to think—that of utilizing the course of study as a principal instrument of indoctrination for music education.

Promptness and Reliability

The daily schedule of the music supervisor must to some extent be a variable one. Special rehearsals for concerts and operettas, additional instruction for certain pupils, performances before community organizations, preparation for many school activities, conferences with classroom teachers—all of these and many other such duties cannot be charted ahead of time for the entire school year. Yet the music supervisor must keep in mind that his own schedule does have a direct bearing upon the schedule and work of many other people in the school system.

Miss Williams could not prevent it this morning when the high school assembly ran well overtime because of a long-winded speaker. She had to stay to the end to lead the final song. Just the same, Miss Meyers in the third grade at Jefferson School was expecting her at ten-thirty and had her day's work planned accordingly. Miss Meyers was decidedly out of humor when Miss Williams finally arrived about eleven o'clock.

Last week when the high school choir sang at the Kiwanis

Club meeting at noon Miss Williams couldn't predict that the luncheon schedule was so poorly arranged that all the choir members would be late to their one-fifteen classes. Some of these incidents cannot be prevented and the supervisor is sometimes hard put to make sufficient explanations and apologies. He wants the classroom teachers to co-operate with him and he knows that they can easily become antagonistic toward him and his work if his tardiness and his absence disrupt their own programs.

When the supervisor finds that some unforeseen circumstance is going to prevent his maintaining his schedule he should immediately send word to the other instructors and students whose schedules will be disrupted by his change in plans. This will establish him as a considerate person who is thoughtful of other people. It will assist him in securing future cooperation from those people affected. It is a combination of good manners and good business.

If a school band or orchestra or choir is to appear before a community group it is highly necessary that careful plans be made to make certain that the performance will be on scheduled time. A supervisor who forgets or neglects such an appearance or who arrives late for it is doing severe damage to himself in the community.

Tens of thousands of students are now participating every year in hundreds of district, state, and regional festivals and competitions. The committees who manage these affairs spend much time and energy in making the necessary arrangements and schedules. After a supervisor has signified an intention to enter individuals or groups in such events he should observe carefully the rules and instructions as to time and place. If it is found at the last minute that some of the entries cannot attend, the committee in charge should be noti-

fied immediately by telephone or telegraph. Otherwise there
is likely to be confusion and inconvenience in that positions
may be held in the festival groups for people who will not
arrive, or judges may wait to evaluate the work of people who
will not be there to sing or play. It is not an overstatement
to say that the professional reputations of many supervisors
have been damaged, and in some cases severely, by their failure to co-operate with committees who have worked long and
hard to provide opportunities for their pupils to participate
in these organized affairs.

The Budgeting of Time

Which activities of the music supervisor are really important and which are relatively unimportant? No categorical
answer can be given to this question and none is attempted
here. If, for instance, a supervisor comes into a community
which has emphasized the prominence of the high school band
and finds that the band has been the most important work of
previous supervisors he would indeed be foolish to pay little
attention to the band and interest himself principally in some
other organization.

Speaking from an entirely practical standpoint, the supervisor must be guided to a great extent by existing circumstances and the general cross section of existing interests and
opinions of his school and community. At the same time a
good music supervisor must function as a real *educator* and
utilize every means at his command to provide a *balanced*
program of music education. It may be necessary for him to
begin his work with an unbalanced program, but that is no
excuse for his continuing in the same manner year after year.
Here are three examples of unbalanced programs:

1. The supervisor here was trained primarily as a grade teacher and supervisor. She has had little and poor preparation in the instrumental field. The grade school singing is excellent but all organizations in the high school rank low in performance standards.

2. The high school band in this community has driven all other music activities out of the picture. The supervisor does not even visit the grades. He leaves all instruction there in the hands of the classroom teachers. Much money has been spent on band uniforms and instruments. The supervisor's time is spent almost entirely on wind and percussion training. The two high school glee clubs, with very small membership, each learned about six new selections last year.

3. This supervisor spends nearly all his time in training an a cappella choir. The instrumental work is very poor. Grade supervision is half-hearted and consists mainly of "scouting" for better voices that can be prepared and trained for the high school choir.

It is not in the province of this book to deal with those matters and problems which lie more strictly in the fields of music education theory and practice. There is no intention here to outline what may be considered a well-balanced music education program with proper allocation of time and effort to the many aspects of music education such as kindergarten training, elementary vocal work, rhythmic activities, listening activities, integration, piano class instruction, band and orchestra instrumental training, voice classes, theory classes, etc.

Our purpose in examining the problem of balance of these various fields of activity at this point is to emphasize the relation of proper balance to the general stability and strength of the entire program. It is dangerous to depend too much upon some single organization or type of work such as band or orchestra or chorus for continued community support. Some one organization may be raised to outstanding ability and prominence. The supervisor's security and that of his work may safely rest upon this one activity *for a limited time*. It is possible to develop almost astonishing community support for some group which has been well trained and publicized. But this "fever-heat" support, without the backing of a well-balanced general music education program, is dangerous in the same manner that a highly successful football team can be dangerous to a physical education program which has neglected the interests and needs of the great majority of pupils in a school system.

It is good business for the music supervisor to budget his time and efforts so that his success and reputation will not be dependent upon only one or two organizations. What is more, it is a sound plan for good music education. In recent years the tendency of many supervisors to spend almost all of their time and effort upon a few "show" groups has greatly weakened the more democratic aspects and functions of public education as applied to music. It is generally estimated that only approximately 15% of the high school students throughout the country take some active part in the high school music curriculum. This is dangerous and it leaves our whole program and profession in a very vulnerable position. The other 85% of these students are going to take their places in their communities and become citizens and taxpayers. It is entirely reasonable to believe that 85% of the school board members of the future will be people who had no contact with music above the "required" point in seventh or eighth grade. And there is no reason to assume that the music experiences of the **85% while they were in elementary and junior high school** were particularly satisfactory, what with the great number of music supervisors who have come to neglect this more democratic field in favor of the selected 15% who enter into groups that are capable of producing superior public performances.

The foregoing remarks should not be construed as criticism or undervaluation of highly skilled special groups. There is constant and continuing need for more groups of that kind—groups which can command respect for the quality of their performances. The cause of music education needs more of them. They can act as the spearhead of influence through their superior performance achievements. But it is well always to remember that these groups include only a limited portion of the school population. Where are the other pupils?

What is the effect of too much "specialization" upon the professional career of the young supervisor? It works against him when he attempts to secure larger supervisorships and directorships which require a working knowledge of the whole field of music education. In recent years there has been a considerable tendency, particularly upon the part of young men who are starting out as music supervisors, to avoid positions in smaller towns where there is only one supervisor who must do all work, vocal and instrumental, and to seek specialized positions where the sole requirement is band, orchestra, or choir conducting. After acquiring some years of experience many of these instructors have applied for full supervisory or directorship positions only to find that for those jobs school administrators favor candidates who have better balanced and wider experience.

The supervisor owes a balanced budget of time and effort to his school and community and to himself. If he does not develop it he will risk the loss of future community support and the possibility of finding himself unable to advance.

Planning for Personal Life

In the preceding paragraphs of this chapter the discussion has had to do with the organization of the daily work of the supervisor in the classroom and the community functions of his groups.

It seems safe to say that most people, in looking back upon the experiences of their schooling, turn their first and warmest thoughts upon the *teachers* who made things worth-while rather than upon the subject matter content of courses. Good teachers must be real people and if they are going to be *real* they must do something besides teach.

The relation of the music supervisor to the community was treated in Chapter III and there is no need to repeat that material here. However, there is need for continued emphasis upon the necessity for the music supervisor to spend some of his time—a reasonable amount—with the people of his community in their normal ways of living in the American scene. A well-conceived budget of the supervisor's time must include some activities which have nothing to do wth music and the schools. He must find time to be a real citizen; to be interested in the general affairs of his community apart from music and education; to live with other people as if he were a merchant, a doctor, a farmer, or a mechanic; to have a concern for current social, economic, and political problems; to play a part in community life other than the role of teacher; and to keep himself balanced in his interests.

Chapter 6

PURCHASE OF SUPPLIES AND EQUIPMENT

LARRY RHODES has just left Superintendent Decker's office and is heading toward the music room. He's moving slowly and without the usual spring in his step. Everything about him looks dejected.

He meets Clem Fletcher, a commercial department teacher, in the corridor.

"Hello, Larry."

"'Lo, Clem."

"Say, what's the matter? You certainly are not a very happy looking specimen this morning."

"Well, who would be after what I've just been through?"

Clem had seen Larry come out of Mr. Decker's office.

"In trouble with the boss?"

"No . . . and yes. He's all right even though he did give me a little talking-to this morning. He's on my side, in a way, but the real trouble is with the board of education—after what they did again last night."

"So? What did they do?"

"They turned me down again on a lot of things I need."

"That's the second time they have done that, isn't it?"

"Worse'n that—the third time."

"There must be something wrong somewhere because this town's not broke. Look at the other stuff they've been buying recently."

"Clem, that's just what's bothering me. I know they have the money. I know I need everything I've asked for. But, somehow or other, I just don't seem to be able to get it. You have a free period now, haven't you? Come on into my room and look this over and see if you can find the answer."

They sit down in the music room and Larry hands to Clem a sheet which contains a list of materials which he has asked the board to purchase for him—a list of music, instruments, books, etc. Clem studies it.

"Well, Larry, I don't know anything about music so I don't know how important some of these things are. I suppose you need an oboe and a bassoon but you couldn't prove it by me. I don't think you would ask for all these grade school books unless you have a good reason, but they do mount up to a sizeable figure."

"*Do* we need an oboe and a bassoon? *Do* we need new grade books? *Do* we? How in the world can an orchestra or a band go to a competition and make a good . . ."

"Whoa, fellow! I'm not the board of education. You don't have to sell *me*. It's the board that you've got to convince."

"That's what Mr. Decker said this morning."

"Maybe there's your answer. Have you sold anyone except yourself on all these things before asking for them?"

"*I* ought to know what we need. After all, I spend my entire time teaching music and they should be willing to take my word on things like these."

"Yes, I know. But remember that it's the taxpayers' money they are spending, not yours. Let me ask you a few questions, Larry. Have you really done anything to make Mr. Decker and the board members see the need for all these items before asking for them?"

"Well . . ."

"I'll bet you haven't and that there's your trouble."

"Mr. Decker said something like that."

"What did he say?"

"He said that the board members felt that they couldn't spend all this money without first knowing more about why they should spend it. He said that some of them laughed at the word 'oboe' and said that they had enough 'hoboes' around town; that they could get a lot of them free. It doesn't mean anything to them that when we entered our band in the district competition last spring I had to have a clarinet play a solo that belonged to the oboe and it practically ruined the effect of the whole number. Then he said, too, that they knew there were a lot of good music books now in the elementary school and they didn't see any need to buy new ones. Yes, they're *good* all right, that is they still have backs on 'em! But I'll bet that some of the board members sang out of those same books when they went to school."

"Now, come on, Larry. I'll bet you haven't told me the most important thing which Mr. Decker said to you."

"Well, he did say, and rather plainly, too, that I would have to make a better case for this list before it would be passed."

"Have you ever sat down with Mr. Decker and told him all the arguments for purchasing these items? Have you ever written out these arguments so that Mr. Decker could hand them on to the board?"

"I've told Mr. Decker we needed all these things but I don't think I ever went into detail."

"Well, then, how did you expect Mr. Decker to make a case for your requests to the board when you had not made your case to him? You give Mr. Decker the right dope on all this and I'll bet he can get the money for you. If he can't do it himself he may ask you to come to a board meeting and present your own arguments. Now let's take a sheet of paper and make a few notes. First . . ."

So Clem Fletcher gives Larry Rhodes his first lesson in the making of a request for materials and the building of a frame of mind for its reception.

Anticipation

Is Larry planning his program of music instruction well in advance? Does he know what he wants to do next year, and the next, in establishing new activities and organizations? Can he see his program unfolding gradually and naturally and with purpose and control? Or will it be simply a haphazard growth subject to circumstances?

Will Larry "time" his new ideas so that they will come before the school and the community when other affairs will not overshadow them?

Will he plan his new ventures so that they will be well distributed and give proper relative emphasis to vocal and instrumental music and to the elementary school, junior high school, and senior high school?

Will he see that his projects are evenly spaced over a period of time so that he does not make too great demands upon the schools, the teaching personnel, the pupils, and the community at any one time? Will he avoid being criticized by his fellow workers for trying to develop too many music ideas at one time for the good of the school system?

If Larry works out these questions in his own mind well in advance he will have made his first important step in insuring the eventual purchase of material which he will need in the future.

If he cannot anticipate his needs well before the time he has to make them known he will hardly be in a good position to conduct a successful campaign for them.

Preparation

Now comes the second step—that of showing the need for the items which will eventually be requested, and of selling the idea to those who are concerned.

Mr. Decker is accustomed to members of his teaching staff coming into his office and asking for supplies of one kind or another. He knows that a lot of people want a lot of things. The question is how much do they *need* them? He is always a little suspicious of teachers who rush into his office with "emergency" needs. If these teachers are planning their work in advance, as they should be doing, just how do these "emergencies" develop?

Last week he knew that Larry had a real emergency on hand when one of the school's two cellos suffered an accident and had to be repaired in time for a concert. But he can't quite get it through his head why Larry is in such a big rush to purchase an oboe and a bassoon, both of which look like rather expensive items. If these instruments are so important why hasn't something more been said about them before this time?

When Larry presented his list of needs to Mr. Decker he took little or no time to explain it or to give reasons why various items were included. Mr. Decker was in a hurry at the moment and simply slipped the list into a folder with other appropriation items to be presented to the board. At the board meeting he presented the music list along with others and suddenly found himself confronted with a lot of questions to which he did not know the answers. He now feels that Larry was responsible for his discomfiture because he failed to provide the necessary background and facts.

If Larry knows now that next year he will ask for an expensive tuba, a new piano for the music room, a set of phonograph records for junior high school classes and an ample addition to the high school chorus library, he will do well to begin to "set the stage" now. The first time he mentions any of these items to Mr. Decker it will be a mention and nothing more. A little later he will see another opportunity to put in a good word. During the coming year he will watch carefully for further opportunities to indicate how the work of the music department would be better if only he had such and such items. If he does this well and carefully Mr. Decker is likely to take a real interest and before long begin to feel that *he* wants to see these items in the schools as much as Larry does.

Some day Mr. Decker may ask Larry to go downtown and talk to the president of the school board and tell him how the music work will be bettered if certain purchases are made next year. When and if Larry does this he must be certain that he puts his case so that a non-musician will understand it. His presentation must be practical and businesslike.

Here is an effective way of securing community attention and support but it must be done *very carefully*. If Larry has real needs in the way of music, books, and instruments those needs will be felt in the classroom. If the band sounds bad at times because of incomplete instrumentation Larry can drop a few hints to the band members that if certain other instruments were present the music would sound much better. The tone of a poor piano or phonograph is noticeable to pupils and needs only brief mention once in a while. If a class is weary of singing out of the same book that their older brothers and sisters sang out of years ago Larry can remark, but not too often, that he hopes they can have some new books some day.

If pupils sense the need of new supplies and equipment they

will do something about letting their parents know that the music at the school would be much better if a little money were spent in this direction or that.

However, Larry must never make remarks which could be interpreted as discontent or growling on his part and most certainly never as an alibi for poor musical results.

Every school system has its own peculiar construction and personnel problems which require individual treatment. Only a few generalizations and specific suggestions are possible here. But one thing is certain. If Larry wishes to have immediate and willing approval of his next year's budget requests he had better conduct a good educational campaign *this* year.

On Being Businesslike

The school system's financial routine. Every school system has a definite plan for the purchase of supplies and equipment. A new supervisor should study this plan and learn how it works. He should do so soon after he enters the system. An early understanding of it will save him a lot of trouble and worry.

Too many people have believed that musicians and others who have to do with the arts are necessarily fools when it comes to business and money.

A music supervisor who establishes himself as an intelligent and efficient business person will accomplish something of great value to the music program and to himself. Administrators become weary of dealing with music instructors who insist on following harum-scarum procedures of their own rather than adhering to the general routine established for the entire school system.

It is unfortunate but true that many administrators have stated that their music instructors have caused more disruptions in their administrative routine than all other teachers combined.

If the superintendent personally handles all matters of budget, requisitions, and orders, the supervisor should sit down with him and learn the rules. If the clerk of the board of education, or a business manager, or some other official is in charge of matters financial, then the supervisor should go to him and say, "I want you to explain your rules and routine to me so that I shall be able to do things the way that you want them done."

When a music supervisor is doing business he should act like a businessman, not like a musician. Promptness, reliability, accuracy, neatness—all these and many other qualities which are a part of good business procedure are just as valuable to the music supervisor as they are to the merchant, the lawyer, the banker, or any other businessman.

Budgeting. Nearly all school systems are operated on a budget which is planned and formulated well ahead of the time of its adoption. This budget deals with anticipated revenue and expenditures for the year ahead. The principal part of its preparation is generally done by the superintendent of schools in co-operation with the financial officer of the board of education.

It is usual to ask department heads, such as the supervisor of music, to list and estimate the expenditures necessary for the coming year. As mentioned previously in this chapter, those items requested by the music supervisor should have been planned well ahead of time and prepared for in such a way that they are likely to receive friendly consideration by the members of the board of education.

Some supervisors follow the policy of asking for many more items than they expect to receive so that, after their requests have been reduced in final trimming of the budget, they will eventually come out with just about what they really wanted in the first place. Sometimes this strategy works, but it should be kept in mind that any request which is out of reason and proportion faces a possible total defeat because it may appear that the person who made it was without reason and balance.

Knowing the market and sources of supply. Every supervisor should have an extensive file of catalogues of books, music, instruments, uniforms, and other essential materials.

A superintendent respects a supervisor who comes to him and says: "Mr. Decker, we need so-and-so. I've been investigating and I find that there are several firms which produce this article. I have obtained all the literature I can and have read it carefully. I've also asked other music supervisors what they think about the several brands. Taking all data into consideration I've decided that this one is the best buy. Here is a sheet on which I have written the details concerning each brand, also the information about cost."

Mr. Decker knows that cost is an important item only when considered along with many other factors. Many times the cheapest articles are in the long run the most expensive from a practical point of view. At the same time he hopes that his supervisor of music has done the best he can in finding an article which will provide the most for the money spent.

The supervisor should select his materials with care and study. He should know *why* he is recommending the purchase of a certain article. Many requests have been rejected simply because they have seemed to have no background of objective thinking and evaluation.

Decisions to purchase music, instruments, and books should not be hurried. They should be deliberate and studied.

Purchase Procedures*

Requisitions. Because of budget requirements and bookkeeping a school system may require the filing of an official requisition form before any purchase machinery may be started. If that requisition draws from funds which have been allocated to the music department in the budget it can be issued and signed by the supervisor. If it calls for materials which normally are charged to some other section of the budget allocated to the high school, elementary schools, etc. the requisition must be issued by the person responsible for that section.

Sometimes this kind of requisition is merely a matter of bookkeeping and is taken care of by an administrative official upon request, oral or written. In nearly all cases it needs the approval of the superintendent.

Purchase requisitions. Many boards of education instruct firms with whom they do business to refuse to fill orders unless those orders are accompanied by an official requisition for purchase. This pratice is intended to prevent the filling of

---

*The Music Education Exhibitors Association, an affiliate of the Music Educators National Conference, has published an official Conference bulletin entitled *The Business Handbook of Music Education.* It deals extensively with the relation of the music educator to the firms who supply the materials and services of music education. In this pamphlet will be found many helpful suggestions concerning correspondence and personal acquaintance, accounts, orders, shipping instructions, copyright, specifications of music instruments and uniforms, teachers agencies, etc. It also contains a list of the current members of the Music Education Exhibitors Association, together with their addresses and a brief summary of their principal products and services.

Copies of this bulletin may be secured without charge from the headquarters office of the Music Educators National Conference, 64 East Jackson Blvd., Chicago, Ill.

unauthorized orders and to insure proper budget control and bookkeeping.

Sometimes the music supervisor may have immediate need for some item and feel that he cannot wait for the usual routine to be accomplished. He may then get in direct touch with the firm and ask that the material be sent before the firm receives the official requisition. If this procedure is found necessary the supervisor should make certain of the following: (1) that his action has the approval of the superintendent; (2) that the requisition will be sent promptly; and (3) that the requisition will be accompanied by a note which states that it is for material already shipped, otherwise a busy order department may send a duplicate shipment. Another way of handling this kind of transaction is for the supervisor to charge such material temporarily to his personal account and then have it transferred to the school account when the official requisition is available.

Each board of education has its own method of doing business and it is imperative that the supervisor understand and follow that method.

Orders. Every firm wishes to fill orders promptly and accurately. Many delays in the filling of orders are directly attributable to the music supervisor himself because the information which he provides is inaccurate or insufficient.

In ordering music and books it is necessary that accurate and specific information be given concerning titles, names, authors, kind of arrangement, edition, number, high voice, low voice, small orchestra, large orchestra, full band, symphonic band, and so on and on.

How is an order clerk to know what to send when he sees an order for "10 copies—The American Song" when he knows that this one composition is available for high, medium, and low voice, SAB, SSAA, SATB and also as a piano number? What does he do? He has to lay the order aside and someone must write a letter to find out what the customer really wants. In the meantime the customer is probably complaining about the poor service of the firm.

It is well to write orders for printed materials with copies of those materials close at hand so that all necessary information can be taken directly from them. Much time, worry, and inconvenience will be avoided if this practice is followed.

In purchasing supplies and equipment such as musical instruments, uniforms, and accessories, the order should indicate specifications such as model numbers, materials, finishes, size, color, and other qualifications which apply.

The purveyor is eager to have his service efficient and satisfactory. He will do his best. But if he were to be frank and honest, he would say that the majority of mistakes in the filling of orders are due to carelessness and inaccuracy on the part of the customers. And, in the end, the customer is the one who is most inconvenienced by his own negligence.

"On-approval" orders. An "on-approval" charge is a definite obligation to the customer just the same as is any other purchase. There is no ethical reason to regard material received "on-approval" as something which can probably be kept but not paid for, provided the bills are ignored long enough. When a customer writes "Please send me so-and-so 'on approval'" he should expect to *pay* for that item unless he returns it, in salable condition, within the time limits allowed by the vendor.

If a firm is willing to send its materials "on-approval" and to assume the expense of those transactions, it is only reasonable that it should expect the customer to pay promptly for items which are retained and to do so without the necessity of a series of "duns" which involve so much work and postage that the whole affair results in a loss. When specific items are ordered "on-approval" it is expected that a percentage of them (each firm has its own policy) will be kept and paid for. When a general request for "on-approval" material is made the customer should describe as accurately as possible the needs which it must meet so that the firm will have at least a reasonable chance of sending material which will be retained and paid for.

Accounts. Larry Rhodes will have occasion to order materials for his own use—items which are not to be paid for by the board of education. Perhaps he will wish to open personal charge accounts with several firms. He should arrange for the opening of these accounts in advance of the time when he expects to use them. In making these arrangements he should present the names of several suitable references.

Most important of all, he should expect to pay his bills promptly. These accounts are carried for the convenience of the customer so that he may make a monthly settlement for a number of transactions. They are not for the purpose of extending long-term credit. The way to avoid credit troubles is to keep accounts paid up and not let charges accumulate.

If Larry orders some music for one of his pupils and has the charge placed on his account he should collect from the pupil promptly. After making that collection he will do well to keep the money apart from his own personal funds, otherwise he may spend it and then wonder at the end of the month how he is going to balance his accounts. Larry should always remember that he—not his pupils—is responsible for charges that have been placed on his accounts. It is unfair for him to ask firms to extend credit indefinitely just because he cannot make prompt collections from his pupils.

Separate accounts. When Larry orders items which are to be charged to his personal account he should word his order so that the charge will be made properly. He should include some statement such as "Charge to my personal account." If he is ordering for an organization account or for a high school account, some definite notation should be included so that it will be plain where the charge is to be placed.

Professional Ethics

Should the music instructor accept commissions on materials used in his music education program? To this question should come a unanimous, firm, and unequivocal answer of "NO." That should be the answer if we believe that music education is truly a profession and not merely an occupation which enables us to snatch dollars without respect for ethical considerations and good taste.

Our approach to this question should not be one of taking refuge in legal arguments, or of justifying ourselves because we need to earn more money, or of scheming to see what we "can get by with." Rather, it should be a clean-cut wish to take the position that we are possessed of some ideals in the choosing of a profession and that we are now willing to live upon our *professional* incomes and steer clear of shoddy "on the side" deals which look at least slightly off-color.

If Bill W. is receiving commissions on materials sold to his pupils or his schools who does he think is *really* paying those commissions? Does he think that the vendor is paying them to him? What a ridiculous thought! Of course the vendor isn't making any contribution of that kind. The pupils or the school is paying an extra large price in order to give Bill his "cut." Bill should never deceive himself on that point. The fellow who offers him commissions isn't going to *pay* them. Not at all. He merely sets his price so that he will have extra profit to give to Bill for his part in the deal.

So, when Bill consoles himself with the thought that some businessman or some distant concern is shelling out some extra money for him, he is either ignorant or is closing at least one eye to the ethics of the situation.

If Bill takes commissions he must realize that they are paid by the people of his community, the people who hired him to come into their schools and community to guide a program of music education. When he signed his contract he took upon himself the responsibility for that program. His contract is not a license to set up a profitable business on the side.

Suppose Bill says "Well, I help all these kids select their instruments. It takes a lot of my time. I have to do a lot of correspondence and extra work for them and the school board. Why *shouldn't* I get something out of it?" The answer is that all the things which Bill regards as "extra" work are really a part of his job and he should so consider them.

If Bill gets into the commission game he will forget his rationalization about accepting the fees on the basis of investment of extra work and time. He will soon come to think of this income in a matter-of-course manner and as something that is due him. Then he approaches a situation that might just as well be described as out-and-out graft. Why? Because he will be influenced in his choice of brands by the relative sizes of the commissions offered.

Suppose Bill's bank account is a little low this month. A nice order of new materials is to be purchased by his pupils or his school. Several vendors come along. Some offer Bill larger commissions than others. What is Bill likely to do? The very fact that Bill is involved in commissions *at all* makes us doubt immediately the sincerity of his eventual decision.

A firm stand on this matter should not come from a fear of getting caught but rather from a positive determination to keep clear of deals which, by all good standards, violate good professional conduct. But if one who is tempted lacks the necessary ethical outlook, what are the more practical factors which should be sufficient to keep him on the right path?

First, if Bill ever has a part in a secret or questionable deal there is always at least one other person who knows about it. That means that there is someone whom Bill must fear; someone who can harm him if he doesn't keep on with the same kind of deals; someone who can damage his future and career; someone who can tell him what to do—or else.

Second, school administrators have a way of knowing when secret deals are being made, even though they do not have proof that would stand up in court. Just because Bill's superintendent doesn't accuse him of these deals doesn't mean that he does not know what is going on.

Third, the news will travel. Deals that are "secret" do not stay secret. If Bill is involved in some questionable deals it is inevitable that he will be classed with those in the profession who have a reputation for hard-boiled money grabbing rather than for educational advance.

Some instructors may justify their commissions on materials sold to pupils on the grounds of services rendered. We still believe that a contract with the board of education implies those services as a part of the duties of the position. Regardless of that argument, there is a very insidious aspect to this practice. Those who begin to take commissions on material sold to pupils many times begin to look longingly at the possibilities for similar commissions on material sold to the boards of education who employ them. They begin to feel that they should make a profit on *all* material which is selected by them.

On this question of commissions on materials purchased by the schools *there is no compromise*. The practice is not only unethical, it is downright dishonest. It is bribery—and there is no other word to describe it accurately. Should the janitor get a "rake-off" on the coal he uses in the school furnaces? Certainly not. Should the office secretaries receive "cuts" on the typewriters and office supplies which they use? Should the science teachers receive commissions on laboratory equipment? Should the history teachers profit on the maps and books that they use? To all of these questions the answer is obviously "No." The same goes for music supplies.

Someone may now present the case of the town with no music dealer and with no dealer located near by. The music instructor does not wish to have his pupils order their supplies by mail. He knows that they need his advice and counsel. So, he assumes the work and responsibilities which are usually a part of the dealer's business. Now, should he be permitted to take the commissions which would ordinarily go to a dealer?

We believe that there is a direct and simple way to answer that question. If that instructor is willing to be a dealer in the out-and-out sense and if he has the authorization of his board of education and the approval of his community, he may proceed safely. He can say to himself, "I would be willing to see a record of all my transactions printed on the front page of the local paper. I am willing to have all people in the community know that I am making profit on these sales." Anyone who cannot say those things to himself is courting trouble.

However "right" the instructor may be in his handling of commercial deals we firmly believe that the profits which he derives from them are small in proportion to the eventual cost to his professional career. The individual who uses his music teaching position as a basis for small money-grabbing schemes of one kind or another is not likely to attain professional leadership and standing of first rank.

It must be remembered that school administrators shy away from teachers who are involved in commission schemes. They do not want them in their schools. They are distinct liabilities and are always likely to cause trouble in the community. Many, many case histories could be presented to prove this contention.

This commission racket cannot be dismissed by laying it at the doors of the people who offer the commissions. It must be decided by the professional people themselves and upon the basis of high professional standards.

Chapter 7

CORRESPONDENCE AND RECORDS

Good Manners

Would Lewis Bailey go to a business appointment in a wrinkled suit, a soiled shirt with no tie, and muddy shoes? Certainly not. He would consider an unkempt appearance an uncomplimentary gesture in the direction of the person with whom he had the appointment.

But Lewis has just finished doing something very much like that. He has written a letter. And what a letter! For stationery Lewis used a soiled sheet of theme paper which some student had dropped in the music room. Not having a typewriter or pen and ink close by, he decided that it would be all right to write with a pencil. As for form, it looks terrible! The handwriting? Hardly legible. Neatly folded for the envelope? Of course not. Now the person who receives that letter will very quickly form a mental picture of Lewis and his habits. What kind of picture will it be? The answer is obvious.

Correspondence is a substitute for personal contact. All the niceties and manners of personal relations apply to correspondence also.

Promptness

Let's make another parallel concerning Lewis' letter. Would Lewis feel that it was perfectly all right to be two or three hours late to an appointment? No. Then why does he feel that he can afford to be dilatory in his replies to letters? Again, the same rule of good manners applies.

Prompt replies to letters are appreciated. Very well, let Lewis be prompt in his replies and he will make friends.

Stationery

Individual and personalized stationery is available at little cost. Letterheads giving the name, location, and position of the writer make a good impression and are of value to the reader in that they show immediately the name and business of the writer. Any print shop will be glad to assist in the designing of attractive correspondence forms.

A word of caution! Stationery that is for purely personal use, as contrasted with professional use, need give only the name and address of the user. However, on stationery for professional use the name of the individual should not be more prominent than that of the institution or the school system in which he is employed.

If Lewis Bailey wants some professional stationery for his use as supervisor of music in the Bordenville schools he should not place his name in the largest type in the center of the page. After all, the Bordenville schools are more important than Lewis. Perhaps it would be well for him to use somewhat the same style of letterhead as that used by the central school office, adding his name and position in reasonably small type at the left-hand side of the page, well toward the top. Any good printer will know how to do this for him.

And under no conditions will Lewis place B.S., M.A., or Ph.D. after his name. The listing of degrees on professional stationery simply isn't done.

If Lewis is at all doubtful regarding how much prominence he should give to his own name he should err on the side of underemphasis.

Form

In considering form, let us think first of the general appearance of the letter rather than of its technical features. As the page is unfolded does it present an attractive appearance? Does it give an impression of careful composition and writing or does it indicate that the writer is slovenly and careless? After the writer has finished a letter, folded it and placed it in the envelope, let him take it out of the envelope, unfold it and see what kind of an impression it makes on *him*. We believe that a lot of letters would be rewritten if this were done.

There is no need to discuss here the many mechanical points of letter writing. Every person who has completed a college course has had training along that line—in elementary school, in junior high school, in high school, and again in college. It is not a question of not *knowing* how to write a good letter. It is more a question of *caring* about it.

For a dollar or two a music educator can purchase one of the many good correspondence handbooks which are available on the market—the kind which is used by stenographers and secretaries. These small volumes are complete, condensed, and authoritative. It pays to have one of them around for frequent reference.

Neatness

It sounds like grade school teaching, doesn't it, to talk about neatness in letters? Perhaps so, but if the reader were to look through a large batch of correspondence written by teachers he might erroneously come to the conclusion that the writing had been done by grade school pupils. This is no exaggeration. Since this volume is not being written merely to compliment teachers and teaching, we might as well say that letter writing by teachers, in general, is a sorry business.

Legibility

Perhaps it is not reasonable to expect everyone to produce beautiful script, but it is not too much to expect at least careful script. The first and most obvious answer to the person with poor handwriting is the typewriter. It has been our observation that typewritten letters are the ones first read in any stack of mail. Less legible letters are left for the last.

In writing titles and proper names it is well to print them unless your handwriting is very clear. Be certain to print them if your *o's* look like *a's* and your *w's* like *m's*.

And now for your signature. We realize that it is a grand feeling to finish a letter by signing it with a "personality" signature written with a full flourish. But it is many times difficult for the fellow on the receiving end to read that signature unless he is already acquainted with it. If you are writing on stationery which carries your name in the letterhead you may indulge yourself to great lengths in your signature. But if you are writing on plain paper it is best to sign your name so that it can be read.

Filing Correspondence

A cardboard correspondence file may be purchased for only a few cents. It is a good investment. The habit of "filing" letters in coat pockets, handbags, bureau drawers, and on the piano is not a businesslike one. If you write your letters on the typewriter, carbon copies should be kept; if you write them by hand, you should retain at least a memorandum of the contents of each letter.

Representing You

Your correspondence is your representative. It takes your place in a conversation or an interview. It should possess the same qualities of promptness, reliability, appearance, style, and clarity which you would wish to display in your personal contacts.

So, when you send a letter you can honestly say to yourself, "There *I* go" and at the same time ask yourself if that letter will represent you as you wish to appear.

Records for a Purpose

Why do we say "records for a purpose"? In order to differentiate from records for the sake of records.

There is no doubt that today's music educator does have need for a record-keeping system. The many details which must be watched cannot be kept in mind. They need to be on paper and in such order that they are quickly accessible and accurate.

An inventory of all music supplies should be kept up to date. There should be a record of all school-owned instruments, with information regarding their models, finishes, numbers, original cost, upkeep cost, and similar items. When instruments are assigned to pupils there should be on file some sort of agreement with pupil and parent concerning responsibility for those instruments. Uniforms should be handled in the same manner.

Music libraries should be well catalogued and a careful record should be kept of parts passed out to pupils for home practice.

Membership and attendance records are necessary for all organizations, also for individual pupils in private work.

How Many Records?

Now comes an important point concerning records. On one hand we have the danger of keeping insufficient records to insure proper management. On the other hand there is the possibility of an instructor's becoming so absorbed in record-keeping that he has little time for anything else.

We recently examined the record-keeping system recommended by a band instructor. It would have done credit to a large corporation and certainly would have been almost a full-time job for one person. Some of those records were truly necessary to safeguard the school's property, to insure a smoothly functioning organization, and to keep the instructor up to date on problems of pupil personnel. But many of them could be placed in only one classification—that of an instructor's *hobby* in keeping up an elaborate system of statistics which served little or no purpose for him or anyone else.

The value of any record form can quickly and easily be determined by asking the question "How often do I have need to refer to that kind of information?" If you find that you have frequent need for it then it is best to set up a file. But if it is something which simply looks impressive and like "big business" then you can forget about it.

Chapter 8

PUBLICITY, ADVERTISING, AND PERFORMANCES

Publicity

In all matters which pertain to publicity the essential keynote must be one of adherence to standards of good taste.

Away with the fellow who runs from the railroad station to the newspaper office as soon as he arrives in a new community and who spends most of his time thereafter haunting that office, armed with long accounts of the doings of the music department (with a liberal use of his name) and with a bountiful supply of pictures of his groups and organizations (in which he always appears in the center spot)!

But let's arouse the fellow who has been in a community for some time, but about whom the public knows little!

The supervisor's efforts to obtain publicity concerning music education activities should not be regarded as a bid for personal prominence. The community is spending money for its music program and it should know something about what it is getting in return. Reasonable and tasteful publicity is in order.

You say that the way for the public to know about music activities is through those activities themselves rather than through news items and articles? You're right! That is the first and most important avenue. But it must be remembered that not all people in a community can come into direct contact with all of the work of the music department. The people who did not go to last Saturday's football game enjoyed seeing the pictures of the marching band which appeared in Monday's paper. Only a limited number of parents attended the elementary school operetta two weeks ago, but it was a good idea to let all the people in town know that it took place and that the elementary school is doing good work in music. When the high school choir receives a good rating in a regional competition, unquestionably the entire community will or should be interested.

There is no formula for publicity, its proper amount, or the methods of obtaining it. It is the supervisor's job to study the channels of public information in his community and to make the best possible use of them. He cannot do this by staying all the time in the school building and at his rooming place. He must get out and take part in the activities of the community.

When a supervisor is first becoming acquainted with his community he should avoid too frequent appearances in the public eye. Suppose that the town newspaper mentions his name very frequently during his first few months of tenancy and that he makes many talks before community groups and, in general, receives a large amount of public mention—not only personal mention, but also professional mention of his work. What is likely to happen? People will think that he is a publicity-seeker, and that he and his music program are receiving too much attention. Also, it is difficult to keep public attention up to such a pitch. It will die down sooner or later and it will then be difficult to regain.

The shrewd supervisor will see that items of interest concerning the workings of the music department come before the public at well-timed and properly spaced intervals. He will avoid a veritable barrage of publicity followed by a long period of silence.

Newspapers and Their Staffs

Newspapers are almost universally more than willing to co-operate in providing their readers with educational news. In the first place, the carrying of such news marks a paper as a civic-minded force. In the second place, a good editor recognizes the fact that families like to see the names of their children in print, and the listing of the membership of a school organization or the cast of a school performance offers excellent opportunity to include a long list of names and thereby please many readers.

The average small town newspaper does not boast a staff member who is a specialist in writing on music and music events. The editor and his reportorial staff are usually appreciative of assistance from the supervisor in the preparation of news material concerning music events.

If possible, the supervisor should establish personal contact with some member of the news staff of a newspaper and work through that one person rather than in a general way. Then when he has something of interest to say he can feel at liberty to call or see this individual and tell him what kind of news story he has available. The staff member will appreciate receiving accurate, well-organized information—not an already written story.

As has been said above, newspapers do appreciate assistance and co-operation in the presentation of educational news but, on the other hand, they do not like to be imposed upon and regarded as a free publicity channel for the fellow who wants to see his name in print a lot of times. When a supervisor has once worn out his welcome it will be hard for him to obtain further mention of his work. There is a difference between news and nuisance.

Advertising

When it comes to the advertising of performances for which admission is charged it is unfair to ask newspapers to provide all the advance publicity free of charge. Newspapers receive their chief income from the sale of display advertising space. It is only reasonable for the supervisor to include in his budget for performance costs a reasonable amount of money for legitimate advertising. If he will play fair with the newspaper on this policy the paper will most likely be more considerate of him in the handling of news material.

The publicity-wise supervisor handles his distribution of window cards, posters, and other advertising media with good taste. Too much ballyhoo doesn't give his music program the right kind of standing.

When he is writing copy for display advertising the supervisor might well ask for help from the advertising department of the newspaper. Many times this kind of advertising is ineffectual because of poor copy and layout. It can be made effective if some time and effort are spent on preparation of good copy. If money is spent on this kind of material it should be productive of results in the form of increased ticket sales.

Public Performances

Here we are considering public performances not in the light of their content, quality, or musical and educational values but rather as they function in the business of public relations.

Many people of the community come into their only direct contact with the music education program at these public performances. No matter what kind of day-by-day work is being done at the school, they cannot or do not observe it or know much about it. They are going to make up their minds regarding the worth of the music supervisor on the basis of what they see and hear when they come to performances.

This means that performances of all kinds—operettas, choir and chorus concerts, band and orchestra concerts— must be managed and organized so that the music department will appear to be functioning with a high degree of efficiency.

Has the public been well-informed about this performance, and have preparations been made to secure an impressive and good audience? Or will the audience be a small one and unrepresentative of the community population?

Are intelligent and trained ticket sellers and ticket takers on duty at the door so that the arriving audience immediately sees signs of good organization?

Are ushers at work and do they know how to seat people in a pleasant manner?

Are programs available for everyone in the audience? Are they attractive in appearance? Do they give proper credit to all people who have assisted in making the performance possible, or do they "hog" the credit for the music supervisor?

Does the whole production seem to have been organized with skill, or is it clumsy and halting in its pace?

Has the auditorium been made as attractive as possible, perhaps with the addition of a few extra notes of decoration?

Does the supervisor have everything sufficiently well organized to be able to associate with the audience after the performance rather than having to busy himself with small details with the groups on stage? Here is an excellent opportunity to meet and visit with many people at a most advantageous moment.

These performances are important events for a music supervisor. He is before the public in his official capacity. The audience is in position to make an appraisal of him and his work. So he must carefully plan and execute even the smallest details so that he will be certain of his background and be able to present his best artistic endeavors without worrying about many mechanical problems which can do so much to make or break such an event.

Chapter 9

ASSORTED THEMES WITH BRIEF DEVELOPMENT

Seen in Public

BETTY HAVENS wants to know whether her life is her own or whether it belongs to the people of Bridgeville. She is weary of having people comment on her comings and goings and on her behavior in general. Everyone knows that she is a good music teacher. There is no complaint about her work in the school or with community organizations, but there is an occasional buzz of comment on her personal behavior.

What business is it of the Bridgeville people that she was seen in a not-too-reputable tavern last Saturday night in a town forty miles away? Other respectable and accepted Bridgeville people were there too. Why shouldn't she smoke a cigarette in her car while driving from the High School to the West End School? A number of women in "better class" Bridgeville families smoke in their cars as they drive about town. What if she did arrive home "with the milkman" one Saturday morning recently? Why should these people show so much interest in the out-of-town boys that come to visit her? Why should they ask so many questions when she takes an occasional trip out of town over a week end?

Well, Betty, teachers have been up against questions like these for a long, long time—hundreds of thousands of teachers in thousands of Bridgevilles. It is a tough problem and a delicate one.

111

If you had taken a clerical position in Bridgeville, people would have paid little or no attention to your personal conduct and habits. But you are not working for a private firm; you are working for the community. Yes, we know that the community is probably asking you to live "better" than it does itself, but you must remember that you are expected to be a positive influence in the lives of the young people of the community. In fact, you may even be expected to be a *better* example than their parents. This is perhaps unfortunate, but it is true. And we do not know what you can do about it. We have seen teachers rise up and defy the community but in most instances that has been a suicidal move.

We know of only one successful formula. When you move into Bridgeville you must begin living as Bridgeville does, no matter how much it hurts. Until the people of the community know you well and accept you, your conduct must conform to their standards. Later, after you are well-established, perhaps you can do things a little more your own way.

If you simply cannot get along with the Bridgeville people; if they continue to censure and criticize you; if you are resentful in your attitude toward them, then there is only one thing for you to do. Get out and go somewhere else, and do it before your record of service gets into such condition that it will be a liability instead of an asset in securing future positions.

By the way, it is always well to have some good personal friends in town and apart from the school system. They can keep you posted on your progress in the community.

Concerning Your Predecessor

"The music work here was in terrible shape when I came here this year. You just wouldn't believe how bad it was. I don't know how the supervisor who was here before me spent her time. Honestly, the seventh and eighth grades do not know any more than the primary grades. I asked a seventh grade class the other day how many sharps there are in the key of E, and not a one in the class gave the right answer. As for the instrumental work, you should have seen the violins in the orchestra. Not a one of them even knew how to *hold* his instrument, let alone *play* it. I'm having an awful time trying to teach good tone quality to the high school choir."

And so on and on and on. How many times has this kind of wail been sounded by a supervisor who has recently started on a new job! What a poor impression it makes on the listener!

All the charges may be true, but even if they are it is better not to make them. You have been hired to do the job from this point on, not to complain about the past. Complaints do not carry a good professional flavor. Many times they give the impression that the person who is making them wishes to take some credit in the future at the expense of his predecessor. If nothing good can be said about your predecessor then it is better that nothing be said—and in a nice way, too.

Concerning Your Co-Workers

For the sake of simplicity the contents of this volume have been addressed to a "one-person" music department. Now let's look for a minute at a problem which sometimes arises when the music staff consists of two or more people.

There is nothing which will contribute more quickly or more generously to the discredit of a music department and its program than disagreement and antagonism between members within that department. Administrators become weary and disgusted with quarrels between vocal and instrumental teachers or between high school and elementary teachers. These unpleasant relations cannot be kept secret. Other teachers will learn of them; pupils will quickly catch on; news of the feuds will soon reach the townspeople. Then what kind of case do we have for music in the schools when everyone knows that two music teachers cannot get along together?

It is always well for the superintendent to establish definitely the official relations of members within a department so that opportunity for disagreement will be lessened. If that is not done, a satisfactory working agreement should be made by the members themselves and if there is any disagreement or difference of opinion it should be submitted to the superintendent *immediately* for his decision. Rulings regarding authority should be made before unpleasantness arises.

If it eventually develops that two members of the same department simply cannot work harmoniously together they should refer *official* matters to the proper administrative head and then keep still about their *personal* differences. Bad professional manners are inexcusable.

Most of these disagreements are generally an accumulation of misunderstandings. They can usually be avoided if there is frank and honest discussion of differences of opinions at all times, tempered with tolerance and flexibility.

A Sense of Humor

We do not know whether a sense of humor can be "developed." Maybe everyone is born with a certain amount and it is capable of being increased. Maybe not. That is a topic for the psychologists. But we can say here without fear of contradiction that it is a good idea for you to use all that you have, and use it gladly.

Watch a good clinic leader when he is working hard with a large band, orchestra, or chorus. With almost measured regularity (even though the members of the organization may not realize it) he will drop a remark or do something which will relieve the tension and get a good laugh from everyone.

Follow a good supervisor from room to room and you will notice that she will find several opportunities during each visit to bring forth smiles or out-and-out hearty laughs.

We are not talking here of being just pleasant and polite with a trick smile which can be turned on without effort. We mean that pupils, teachers, and citizens will be favorably impressed with a person who has some zest for living and who can make other people feel that there is really a lot of fun in life.

Personal Finances

Nothing is more dangerous to a teacher in the schools and in the community than a reputation for financial irresponsibility. A bank account which is carefully and efficiently handled and in which a reasonable balance is maintained is one of the best recommendations and references.

Some "don'ts"—

Don't borrow money from other teachers.

Don't be slow in paying your board and room bills.

Don't borrow money from townspeople.

Don't establish accounts at stores in town unless you expect to be able to pay these accounts at the first of every month.

Don't become involved in any time-payment plans unless you are certain that you will always be budgeted so that you can meet payments promptly.

Don't discuss your personal financial problems with other people unless you have real reason to do so.

Don't live and behave in a manner which will lead everyone to think that you are immediately spending every cent that you earn.

If you will establish a bank account and show some sense in handling it, the place for you to secure financial help in an emergency will be at the bank. Should you find it necessary to ask the bank for help, first make certain that your facts and figures will justify your request and not merely show that you are spending more than you earn.

Other People's Money

The question of handling money which belongs to other people and to organizations is discussed at several points in this volume. It is so important that we believe it deserves additional mention.

In the first place, don't handle such money if you can possibly avoid it. Have all financial transactions routed through the superintendent's office, the business manager, the clerk of the board of education, or some other official.

If you find that it is necessary for you to handle operetta funds, instrument payments, uniform money, etc., be certain to keep an accurate and complete set of books so that they will be available for inspection and audit at any time. Furthermore, do not wait until someone asks for an audit. Have audits made regularly and report them to your administrative superior so that no breath of suspicion can ever be directed toward your financial dealings. Whisperings of this kind are very detrimental.

The King's English

A superintendent of schools sat in his office reading letters of application. He was looking for a music supervisor. Finally he decided that Helen Long seemed to be a likely candidate so he telephoned her to ask a few additional questions about her qualifications and with the thought that he would probably ask her to come for a personal interview. Five minutes later, as he replaced the phone on his desk, Helen Long was "out of the race." The superintendent said to his secretary: "I don't think I could stand having her around here. Anyone who will say 'all right-ie' six times in a five-minute conversation would be too much for me."

A liberal use of "un-huh," "okay," "okey-doke," "yep," and other words and phrases of that kind have ruined the chances of many an applicant.

Teacher Cliques

When Mary Warburton came to Dealton to teach last fall her first close personal acquaintances among members of the school staff were a group of a half dozen teachers who eat their meals at Mrs. Shumway's boarding house. When they invited Mary to go to dinner with them at Mrs. Shumway's one evening she was delighted because she wanted to become better acquainted. Well, that was all right. But before she knew it Mary was spending a lot of her time with these same six teachers. Then she found one day that this group had been known as the "Shumway crowd" for two or three years and that because of their staying to themselves and not associating with other teachers they had become unpopular.

Mary is now trying to get out of this situation. If she is

going to work in the Dealton schools from kindergarten through high school she must be on good and equal terms with all teachers. No favorites.

When and if Mary goes into another town to teach she will take her time and use her head to avoid being identified as a member of any of these small cliques.

Contracts

Hazel Monroe has signed a contract with the board of education in Warren as music supervisor for next year. Before she made application in Warren she had applied for the music position in Hartstown. Now she receives a letter from the superintendent in Hartstown saying that the board of education there has elected her to that position—and at a salary $300 higher than is called for in her Warren contract. What will she do?

If she is a smart girl she will stand by her Warren contract *unless* the Warren board is willing to release her from it. She will probably make a hurried trip to Warren and consult with the superintendent and the board. If they agree to release her she can go happily on her way to Hartstown.

If they will not release her at this late date she should make up her mind to do what all honorable people do—stand by her word. Not only that—she will do it pleasantly. She knows that contract-breaking is not professional and she does not want a black mark on her professional record.

Salary

The candidate who is applying for his first position is not in an advantageous position to bargain concerning salary. In most instances he will have to take what is offered. If he feels that the salary offered him is entirely out of line, it might be well for him to consult with the head of his college music department or the placement bureau. They can give him good counsel and perhaps even do some negotiating for him.

When it comes to matters of salary increases or salaries for future positions it is impossible to give general advice and counsel. If Hazel Monroe has been teaching at Hartstown for two years at the same salary figure and now feels that it is time for an increase there is no reason why she should not sit down with the superintendent and discuss the situation with him frankly. We cannot tell her here whether it would be better for her to stay in Hartstown with a $200 increase or move to some new position which will offer her $300 more. She will have to do her own weighing of factors.

In any event, negotiations concerning salary should be made with the superintendent of schools at all times unless he gives definite instructions to take up the question with the board of education or any of its members.

Fashion Notes

A prominent expert on styles for professional women has said:

"Time was when professional women wore the kind of clothes which could almost have been described as uniforms—clothes in which color, fabric, design, and line were given little thought and poor treatment.

"Sometimes only a few slight changes of line or color combinations will make a great difference in appearance.

"There is no need today for a woman with a small salary check to look dowdy or for her appearance to lack snap. If she does, it is because of inertia or lack of imagination. If the lower priced shops from which she ordinarily buys her garments cannot give her good advice and counsel on what she should wear let her save a little extra money once in a while for a visit to a better shop where she can obtain excellent suggestions and ideas about the kind of clothes which 'will do things for her.' A few visits of this kind will give her good training in the selection of less expensive clothes. The same is true with regard to the finding of a right kind of hair 'do.' "

Pupils like to see their teachers well dressed. If you don't believe that they pay attention to your clothes just watch them some morning when you wear a bright and smart new costume to class for the first time. It will help your teaching a lot if pupils like to *look* at you.

Most modern girls of college age have had considerable experience in the selection of clothes but they must realize that as soon as they enter professional life there must be some changes in their wardrobe. The highly informal and nonchalant wardrobe of the campus is not for the teacher. That does not mean that the young graduate is suddenly going to appear in old and drab costumes, but it does mean that she should choose lines and colors which lend more dignity than did the rather extreme transient styles which were so much fun in college.

Clothes for Men

The standard combination of suit, shirt, tie, socks, shoes, and hat for men does not offer opportunities for such radical style changes as do women's clothes. But in spite of this standardization some very peculiar effects can be created.

It doesn't take much difference in a hat to make a man

look plumb silly. Colored shirts are dangerous business unless much care is used in matching them with ties and suits.
Time and thought should be spent in choosing the fabric and
style of a suit. More time should be spent in making certain
that it fits well.

Perhaps the most important considerations in men's cloth-
ing are in the wearing and the upkeep. A stringy or clumsily
knotted necktie can ruin the effect of an expensive outfit. So
can a pair of unshined shoes.

Snap or Slump?

There goes Dan Martin down the street. At the rate he is
going it looks doubtful whether he will last another block.
Shoulders drooping, head hanging, and feet dragging, he presents a picture of everything other than purpose, life, and zest.

Now Dan may be a really fine music teacher. He may have
a very engaging personality to offset his slow moving and
somewhat slouchy movement. But he will always be handicapped by the fact that the early estimates which most people
will form of him will be colored by an impression of incom-
petence and inefficiency.

Irene Wooster is a pretty girl. She has good features and a
good figure. But her posture keeps her from being generally
attractive. Alert and erect posture and carriage are invalu-
able assets in the making of good impressions. Boys and girls
like to look at teachers who appear as if they have some life
in them.

By the way, let's not forget the value of a well-modulated
speaking voice of good timbre. If there is anything a good
music teacher needs it is a speaking voice which does not
annoy his listeners.

Teachers and Pupils—Socially

Rose Benton and Ted Ellis are beginning their music teaching jobs. Both of them are just a little more than twenty years of age. Both are good-looking. Both are energetic and have the usual interests of young people.

When they go into their respective high schools to teach they will not look much older than some of the boys and girls of high school age. Undoubtedly some of the high school boys in Rose's school will be saying: "Gee, have you seen the new music teacher? She's swell. I wouldn't mind going out with her myself."

Over in Ted's school he is going to create quite a commotion among the high school girls. He is older than the high school boys and has been to college. He is younger than the other men teachers in the high school. Certainly more than one girl is saying to herself or to one of her schoolmates, "Isn't he the *best* looking thing you ever saw? Oh, he's wonderful."

Now Rose and Ted are not so far beyond high school age themselves that they will fail to sense what is going on. We can't blame them if they are a bit flattered by it. After all, if they were not the *teachers* of these pupils the age differences would not be sufficient to keep them from having dates with them. But they *are* teachers and that makes a lot of difference.

We cannot expect Ted to be entirely unaffected when, in a chorus rehearsal, he sees a particularly attractive senior girl looking intently at him with an expression which indicates considerable interest—and not just in the music either.

But Rose and Ted are not so foolish as to consider having dates with high school pupils. They know better than that. They are going to handle any "romantic" situations with tact **and a good** sense of humor.

The business of establishing a proper teacher-pupil relationship when the teacher is only four or five years beyond high school age is a serious one. Let's dispose of the "romantic" angle simply by saying that it is "out." There remains the larger and ever-present problem of the teacher being friendly and companionable with pupils, and at the same time retaining the dignity that is necessary if he is to be a good instructor and leader.

None of this business, Ted, of letting high school pupils address you by your first name even though they do it only occasionally and perhaps half in fun. It won't do. Of course, you cannot turn around and say· harshly, "You must say 'Mr. Ellis.' " Your good judgment will dictate a better way than that of handling a delicate situation.

The young teacher can be a strong force in the lives of pupils. Youth is calling to youth in its own language. But as rowdy as youth may sometimes become, it still respects dignity and propriety.

Health and Hygiene

Poor health has blasted many a career which seemed to be on its way to success. The young supervisor, strong and enthusiastic, may depend too heavily upon a youthful body and a good nervous system. It simply does not pay to neglect problems of health with the assurance that they will take care of themselves eventually. They do just that, but sometimes in the wrong way. See a good doctor and a good dentist if only for a routine check-up.

While health complications may many times be unavoidable, there is no excuse for negligence in personal hygiene. Many a candidate for a position has lost out and many teachers in service have lost jobs because of lack of cleanliness and hygiene. We all know what the problems are. It is just a matter of being sensitive to them and developing the right kind of habits.

Don't Break the Law!

Alice Minton mimeographed 300 copies of a copyrighted song for assembly singing last week. Joe Hartwell made an arrangement of a current copyrighted song for a group of students to play at a school party—and without permission of the copyright owner. Helen Owen hasn't had a sufficient number of books for use in her vocal teaching so she has been copying both words and music of copyrighted songs on the blackboard.

All of these people have been breaking the law—just as much so as if they were to steal articles from a downtown store. If we were to accuse them of stealing they wouldn't like it, but the law of the United States Government does protect copyrighted material just as it does other properties.

One general misconception of the copyright law has become rather widespread. It is the belief that the law is not violated if the copies made are not sold for profit. This is not true. Any copying whatsoever of a copyrighted work, without permission of the copyright owner, is a distinct violation of the law. It is punishable with heavy fines beginning at $100, plus minimum damages of $250.

Composers and publishers invest their talent, efforts, and capital in publications. They are entitled to the income from the sale of these items. Any practice which deprives the composer or publisher of just and deserved royalties and sales is an unfair practice.

It is also advisable for the music supervisor to check carefully on the need for permission for public performance of operas and operettas; also on certain larger choral and instrumental works.

Deference to Experience and Age

The young music instructor suddenly becomes a member of that group generally known as the "faculty." That doesn't mean that he can begin calling older and more experienced men "Fred," "Jim," and so on. It will be well to treat these more experienced people with a certain amount of deference and respect. After a time the acquaintance will become closer and more familiar—but this status should be reached slowly and gradually and in such a way that the young instructor has been drawn there, not because he has pushed himself.

Private Teaching

Shall the music supervisor derive additional income by private music teaching? That is a question which cannot be answered categorically. Much depends upon the local situation.

Our first advice is to discuss the matter very thoroughly with the superintendent of schools before making any moves. Find out how many private teachers are already located in the community. What fields do they cover? Will you be damaging the income of citizens and taxpayers whose incomes are dependent upon private teaching? If so, you are on dangerous ground if you enter into competition. Do not enter into private teaching unless you have the approval of your administration.

Competitions

Music educators do not agree upon the value of competition of individuals and organizations in musical performance. In an objective manner we are quoting to you some of the principal points in favor of competition as outlined by a prominent music educator who has managed competitions for many years.

1. Directors have opportunity for comparison of work and exchange of ideas.

2. Expert judges and commentators provide suggestions of great value for future consideration.

3. Competition is a good avenue of development of student motivation.

4. Co-operation of school officials can many times be established most effectively through competition.

5. Better equipment of organizations is sometimes accomplished more quickly when the community realizes that the lack of this equipment has decreased previous competition ratings.

6. Competitions usually are productive of much community support.

7. Students are given opportunity to meet on a democratic basis with pupils of other communities.

8. Since the music performed at competitions must be taken from certain lists there is reason to believe that these lists are made up of better music and therefore increase the quality of music generally used.

9. The spirit of competition is a natural, living thing. Here is an opportunity to compete, but in a manner which must be essentially restrained and in good taste.

To this we might add a few "don'ts" concerning competitions and festivals:

Don't let your pupils take a hard-boiled "win-or-bust" attitude.

Don't complain to judges or committeemen about decisions which have been made.

Don't let your students hear you complain of decisions.

Don't fail to be well-acquainted with the rules and regulations of the competition well ahead of time.

Don't fail to be well-equipped when you are ready to perform—stands, large instruments, music copies for judges, etc.

Don't fail to keep good disciplinary control over students at all times between their departure from home and their return there.

Don't be unbusinesslike in your handling of such problems as transportation, meals, and housing.

Don't fail to learn something from the performance of other contestants.

Don't go home disgruntled if you do not win.

Chapter 10

PROFESSIONAL AFFILIATIONS

An Investment—Not a Gift

"YES, these teachers organizations of one kind or another are all right. I believe in them and I know that they do good. But I already contribute to so many things that I cannot afford to give any more."

This was Dale Haskins' reply to another teacher who had solicited him for membership in one of the several organized teachers groups which play such an important part in the professional advancement of education throughout our country.

Notice that Dale said that he "contributes" in many directions and that he cannot "give" any money to the organized activities of his profession. What mistaken thinking! What a wrong attitude to take!

Dues and payments to these groups constitute an *investment*. They are not gifts.

Suppose that Dale were to become an active member in the following organizations:

1. The Music Educators National Conference (a Department of the National Education Association)
2. A state teachers organization
3. A state music educators group
4. A county music educators association
5. A local group such as an "In and About" music educators association.

His total yearly payment of dues would probably be less than $10.00! What a small part of his yearly salary to pay for the highly valuable services and facilities which these five groups provide! How small is this amount in relation to his income, as compared with the dues which he would pay to his union if he were playing clarinet in a local professional orchestra!

If Dale will set aside only one dollar per month in each month of the school year for his professional affiliation dues he can become an active participant in the maintenance of a national, state, and local structure of educators organizations which exist for the general purposes of educational and professional advancement and solidarity.

Certainly these five affiliations are worth more to Dale than a monthly outlay for two movies or five packs of cigarettes.

Dale should not think of these dues to organizations as "gifts." This is not a matter of charity or benevolence. It is a question of Dale's taking his proper responsibility in the support of practical, effective, and hard-working groups which have been formed to build better and stronger foundations and backgrounds for Dale's profession in general and for his own job in particular. In no way can he purchase better insurance of the future of his job, and for $10.00!

Organizations in American Life

It is natural for Americans to understand and support organizations in American life. A large part of the development and control of social movement, which is politically and centrally guided in many other countries, is here in the hands of groups which have been formed in a co-operative manner. Our member-controlled organizations offer remarkable opportunities for **crystallization and statement of democratic** opinion and action. So long as the members are active in supplying work, thought, and leadership to their own organizations they will have adequate means of expression. Inactivity means the eventual destruction of democratic control.

One of the principal reasons for the prominence of organizations in the American scene lies in the fact that the public realizes that most co-operative organizations have been formed with truly commendable purposes and ideals rather than for purely selfish motives on the part of the members.

Certainly the many teachers associations now in existence represent a large amount of power. But we are not thinking here of "power" in any political sense even though we hold that teachers have the same rights of organization for mutual protection as do any other groups of citizens. Rather we are thinking of the power to advance music in American life—a power which can be demonstrated most effectively through the combination and integration of the activities of tens of thousands of music educators who are now at work throughout the country.

Dale Haskins is now in a profession—the profession of music education. He believes in it. He hopes to be able to make music a more important factor in the lives of many people. Suppose Dale, with his present-day equipment and training, could have miraculously appeared at the turn of the century. Would he have been able to proceed with and accomplish all the things that are possible for him today? Certainly not. Between that day and this the cause of music education has greatly advanced, and much of that advance can be traced directly to the influence of national, state, and local groups of music educators which have been formed to design and construct a sound and effective structure of music education.

In other words, Dale now owes many of his present-day opportunities to those music educators who have worked together to build this structure and to use it in such a way that Dale and fellow members of his profession are now generally accepted and supported by millions of citizens.

Dale is in debt to those who have pioneered in the organization of his profession. His best means of repaying them is now to assume some of their responsibilities and to become active in carrying on the work which they began. He should take his place in the procession of those who have worked long and hard for the cause of music education.

Not Only Dues

Let no one think that organizations in education in general and in music education in particular need only dues in order to carry on successfully. These modest dues are sufficient only to construct a machine for action. They are spent for a variety of items, such as meetings, printing, clerical help, postage, and travel. This machine becomes the vehicle which the educators themselves use in the business of building their program of advancement. Such a machine also may function in a manner which will earn income for the organization far in excess of the total amount of dues paid by the members.

While Dale's dues are of great importance in providing a working machine, there is an even greater need for his personal support and co-operation.

Such words as "support" and "co-operation" are many times given only lip service. They can be said so easily and can mean so little. Here we are talking about active support and co-operation, not passive.

Growth in Service

If Dale Haskins really gets into the spirit of things and becomes an *active* worker in these groups, not only will he make his contribution to the cause, he will receive some of the finest possible training and experience. He will have opportunity to work and exchange ideas with other people who are leaders in the profession. He will grow as a result of these contacts. His vision of the entire field will widen. His perspective upon his own job will become better defined. His maturity and development will be colored and strengthened through his discussions and work with progressive educators from other fields and localities.

It would not be well for Dale to become active in organization work with the principal idea that he will obtain an opportunity to "show off" his talents and personality and thereby attract attention which might assist him in finding a better position. That has been tried, and in most instances the efforts have been so obvious that they have been a deterrent.

However, it should be said that sincere and consistent organization work, motivated by unselfish purposes, has been responsible for the professional advancement of many prominent music educators. School administrators are generally inclined to concern themselves with the record of organization work of candidates whom they are considering for positions. They know that absence of a record of such work is many times indicative of a lack of progressive professional interest on the part of the candidate in his field. At least one teachers' agency regards evidence of good professional affiliations as an essential qualification for those candidates whom it seeks to place. This agency says that lack of such affiliations definitely tends to "lower the stock" of an applicant.

How many times we have heard that statement about people getting out of anything just what they put into it. It is so hackneyed that perhaps we do not pay much attention to it any more. But there is still much truth in it. The people who build and maintain the structures of these organizations are most likely to be the ones who feel the keenest interest and the greatest enthusiasm in their profession. Through this work they will come to know more about their profession and its problems. After they have shown their willingness to serve and their capacities for contribution, they are the people who are most likely to profit.

What Organizations?

The Music Educators National Conference. This is the national professional organization of music educators. With it are directly affiliated such auxiliary groups as the National School Band Association, National School Orchestra Association, National School Vocal Association, and the Music Education Exhibitors Association. Also directly affiliated with it are many of the state associations of music educators, and partial affiliation has been extended to numerous local music education groups.

The National Conference holds a biennial meeting—in even-numbered years. The six Sectional meetings of the National Conference are held biennially in odd-numbered years.

Following is the grouping of states according to the organization of the six Sectional meetings:

Eastern Music Educators Conference: Maine, New Hampshire, Vermont, Massachusetts, Rhode Island, Connecticut, New York, New Jersey, Pennsylvania, Delaware.

Southern Conference for Music Education: Maryland, Virginia, District of Columbia, West Virginia, Kentucky, Tennessee, North Carolina, South Carolina, Georgia, Ala-

North Central Music Educators Conference: Ohio, Michigan, Indiana, Illinois, Wisconsin, Iowa, Minnesota, Nebraska, South Dakota, North Dakota.

bama, Mississippi, Louisiana, Florida.

Southwestern Music Educators Conference: Missouri, Arkansas, Kansas, Oklahoma, Texas, New Mexico, Colorado, Wyoming.

Northwest Music Educators Conference: Montana, Idaho, Oregon, Washington.

California-Western Music Educators Conference: California, Nevada, Utah, Arizona.

The work of these United Conferences must not be thought of only in terms of meetings. The officers, directors, and committee workers of the Conferences, together with the staff members of the Headquarters Office, are constantly carrying on activities which eventually accrue to the benefit of Dale Haskins and his fellow music educators. It is a remarkable tribute to American enterprise and to democratic workings in American education that so many music educators are willing to give so much of their time and energy, and that the administrators to whom they are responsible are willing for them to engage in so many tasks outside their regular daily work.

The young music supervisor in attendance at one of these meetings may think that those people who are elected or appointed to positions of authority and responsibility are merely being honored. Of course there is recognition of ability, leadership, and service in such elections and appointments, but the people who hold such offices must look forward to a period of really hard work. In many instances a person who accepts a major assignment is really signing away all his leisure time and perhaps a part of his regular working time for months to come. Not until one has served in one of these posts does he realize the great sacrifices of time and energy which they require.

When Dale goes to a National or a Sectional meeting he should bear in mind that the program to which he will listen has cost many people a great amount of thought, time, and work. Consultations, letter writing, tedious traveling, trips, telephone calls, disruption of schedules, worries of many kinds, unexpected complications—all these are a part of the building of music education through our conferences. Yet many of those who have served will state emphatically that some of their most important professional growth has come through such volunteer co-operative work.

The Music Educators Journal is the official publication of the Music Educators National Conference and is sent to all active members.

The Research Council is the official research body of the Conference and it is constantly engaged in study of current professional trends. It issues reports from time to time and these are available through the Conference Headquarters office.

Competition-Festivals are sponsored throughout the country by the Conference and its auxiliary organizations—the National School Band, Orchestra, and Vocal Associations.

Outstanding radio programs which serve to present to the public some of the activities of music education in the schools are sponsored by the Conference.

The Headquarters office serves as a clearing house of information concerning many phases of music education and has been of great assistance to a large number of administrators who have requested advice and assistance in starting or developing a music education program.

The yearly dues for active membership in the National and Sectional Conferences are $3. This includes membership in *both* National and one Sectional group for that year and also a subscription to the *Music Educators Journal.*

Other membership classifications are available and information about them may be secured from the Headquarters office but the *active* membership is the one usually assumed by music educators who are in service.

Additional information concerning the activities of the United Conferences and their affiliated groups may be secured by addressing the Headquarters office of the Music Educators National Conference, 64 East Jackson Blvd., Chicago, Ill.

State teachers associations. These associations include teachers of all subjects in their state-wide membership. In some instances the principal state organization of music educators is a part of this general state organization. In others, the music educators group may function entirely apart from or through a co-operative affiliation with the general state organization. It should be remembered by music educators that these *general* organizations are of great value in the maintenance of a strong state program of education. They assume much of the responsibility for legislative activity and for the furtherance of the cause of *all* education. Even though this general organization may not feature a music section as a part of its state program and may leave the chief responsibility for the music program to a separate specialized group, the general association is worthy of active support by music educators because of its guardianship of the entire state program of education.

State music educators groups. These organizations are now a most important part of the national structure of music education. In the new constitution of the Music Educators National Conference, adopted in 1940, these state groups have been given key positions. The meetings of these groups afford excellent opportunities for more personal and intimate discussion and observation in forums, clinics, demonstrations, etc.

The general meetings of these state organizations are usually annual affairs which may be supplemented with special clinics and demonstrations. The dues are small.

Local music educators groups. These groups are sometimes formed as county units or they may draw from an area surrounding some centrally located city or town. Most prominent in their activities are the groups known as "In-and-About" clubs; for example, the In and About Boston Music Educators Club, the In and About Pittsburgh Music Educators Club, the In and About Chicago Music Educators Club, and the In and About Tulsa Music Educators Club. These and many similar clubs draw their membership from the schools of the cities in which they meet and from schools within a reasonable radius of those cities. It is not at all unusual to find people from schools seventy-five to one hundred miles away in attendance at "In-and-About" meetings, which are usually Saturday luncheons.

The programs of these local gatherings are seldom elaborate. They generally include one or two performing groups and one or two speakers. They also provide opportunity for the announcement of important events and performances within the club's drawing area.

Perhaps one of the features of these local meetings most important to the young music educator is the opportunity to meet his fellow workers on a basis that is half professional and half social. Here is a good place to become acquainted and at home in the profession.

City or town teachers' organizations. In small school systems the teachers have adequate opportunities for acquaintance and exchange of ideas with one another in their daily work and in faculty meetings. In systems which include many school buildings there is little opportunity for teachers from different buildings to know each other and to work together except through a local teachers association or club. Certainly the music supervisor will wish to be a part of such an organization.

The Music Teachers National Association. This is a national organization made up principally of private music teachers and music instructors from the faculties of colleges, universities, and conservatories. The meetings are held annually—usually during the Christmas holidays. Some sessions of the meeting are devoted to problems of music education in the public schools, and many public school music educators are members of this organization, in addition to being members of the Music Educators National Conference.

The meetings of this Association will be found particularly attractive to those who wish to hear discussions and demonstrations of more advanced problems of vocal and instrumental teaching, composition, conducting, etc., rather than to those who wish to concern themselves with the more elementary everyday problems of music education in the schools.

How to Take Part

Many a young music supervisor in attendance at meetings during his early years of experience has hoped that the day might come when he could have some part in the activities of professional organizations and perhaps appear on programs as a speaker or demonstrator. That is a perfectly natural feeling. Now what can he do about it?

In the first place he must keep in mind the fact that the people who have charge of the programs and who are appearing on them have arrived at those points gradually and after a substantial period of apprenticeship. Is there any reason for an important organization to summon into a position of prominence a person who has given no indication of ability or of willingness to be of service? If the individual does not first demonstrate his wish to help the organization there is no reason for the organization to reach out to hand him authority or inflate his reputation.

If Dale Haskins really wants to play an important part in some organization he will start at the bottom. He will attend the meetings and take a genuine interest in them instead of hanging around the corridors and lobbies. He will appear early at sessions and help the chairman, if need be, in moving the piano, placing the music stands, carrying chairs, opening windows, passing music, or any other odd jobs which the chairman has on hand—and there usually are plenty of them, with very few people to help.

If volunteers for committee work are requested, Dale should respond, even though some of the jobs may not be very exciting or very important. When he has once accepted assignments of any kind he should carry them through thoroughly, efficiently, and promptly. Conscientious committeemen who can be depended upon are few and far between and committee chairmen are usually more than willing to give them adequate recognition for their efforts.

Much of this matter of growth in organization work is one

of alertness and willingness to do the unwanted jobs while learning what the organization is and how it functions.

Every year hundreds of nominating committees sit for the purpose of nominating people to positions in national, regional, state, and local organizations. Theirs is always a difficult job. Why? Because they know so few people who have *already* demonstrated their ability and loyalty to their organization through willing and competent handling of *lesser* affairs. True, there are many who would be willing to step into the "honor" jobs right off and who feel that they perhaps deserve such positions. But, can a nominating committee make an honest recommendation of such people? Does it dare advance to responsible positions individuals who are really unknown quantities in so far as ability and dependability are concerned? No.

Sometimes the fellow who feels that he is outstanding, even brilliant, in his potential abilities is passed over in favor of the more conservative person who has already demonstrated his values in a quiet way.

Let Dale start in with a local group such as a county association or an "In and About" club. If he will do his work there well and willingly someone will find a way to suggest his name to the leaders of a larger organization and recommend him and his work. If he is willing to "work his way up" he will find his progress assured.

But Dale must be careful not to give the impression that he is out to snatch all the important positions and assignments he can. His sincerity in taking care of his job at hand must always be the thing which is immediately apparent to everyone.

Relatively few people who start out to "politic" themselves into prominent activities and jobs achieve their ambitions. It is true that some of them do, but we must also bear in mind the far larger number who do not succeed because of the bad impressions which they make on the way.

It is no idle statement to say that there are always more important assignments available than there are people who have demonstrated their worthiness for them. If the reader is hesitant to believe this let him talk with some of the people who have been responsible for the programs and activities of some of our important organizations, both large and small. Not that they have found any scarcity of individuals who were willing to take "star" roles—without previous demonstration of ability to fill them—but rather that they have been confronted with a scarcity of people to whom they could give good, solid assignments which require judgment, tact, and experience—the kind of assignments which *must* go to people who have established good records of service and ability.

Attendance at Meetings

Now suppose that Dale Haskins does join several professional organizations and receives from them literature which outlines their plans for the year and lists a number of meeting dates. Is Dale going to try to attend *all* the meetings?

Here is a problem about which few generalizations can be made. Conditions and circumstances are too variable. Here are a few suggestions we should like to make to Dale about his schedule of attendance at meetings.

Make a schedule in advance. Dale should look ahead through the entire school year and make a tentative schedule in advance. This schedule should not call for absence from his regular work too often or too much. Distance of travel and expense must be considered. A balance of the kind of experiences which he will receive should be kept in mind.

Which meetings are likely to give him the discussions and demonstrations which he needs at this time? Which ones will equip him for activities which he has in mind for the future? Will he go to several meetings which will more or less overlap in their content and purpose, or will he distribute his attendance so that he may continue to develop a well-balanced picture of music education? Will he limit his attendance to those meetings which are concerned only with music and music education or will he wish to broaden his outlook through participation in meetings which consider larger educational problems—meetings such as those of the National Education Association, of which the Music Educators National Conference now forms a part? How many meetings can he afford financially? How many days can he be absent from his work?

All of these and many other questions should be studied thoroughly before Dale takes his tentative schedule to his superintendent. When the superintendent asks him questions he must be ready to answer them intelligently and purposefully.

A schedule should be agreed upon early in the school year so that misunderstandings may be avoided later. The superintendent will perhaps advise Dale to cut down or to expand his schedule. The superintendent knows best what the board of education is likely to approve.

Dale must not give the impression that he is eager to go to every meeting about which he hears. He must lead the school authorities and the citizens (who do become suspicious of school people who go to too many meetings) to realize that his attendance at meetings is a truly professional matter and that it is an activity which will result in his becoming better.

qualified to do better music teaching in *their* schools. At this point we are talking primarily about meetings which require some absence from school duties, not dinners, luncheons, week-end, or holiday meetings, which do not affect the supervisor's school schedule.

Budgeting finances for meetings. If a supervisor has made and had approved a schedule for meetings to be attended, he is now in a position to regulate his personal financial affairs in such a way that he can afford the necessary outlay with the least amount of upset in his financial affairs. Saving a few dollars a month ahead of time is a much easier and wiser process than making a severe drain upon any one pay check.

Behavior at meetings. At this point it would be dishonest to evade some plain and straight talk. Americans are "convention going" people. Millions of them go to conventions of all kinds in all parts of the country every year. They all realize that having a good time is an integral part of going to a convention.

No one would wish to make a music educators convention into a solemn, serious, and dull experience with no accent on fun and companionship. Perhaps one of the most serious indictments of the entire teaching profession today is that it lives too much apart from the rest of the world and unlike other people.

But there is the ever-present problem of the music supervisor (and he isn't always a young one!) who takes the attitude that a convention, especially if it is some distance away from home, is a place merely to kick up his heels and have a good time. Programs? Who wants to go to those things? He will read the reports of the meetings later. He's here to see his friends and enjoy himself. Anyway, he's heard all that stuff before.

It is not in the province of this book to pass judgment on this fellow. Maybe he is right. Maybe his few days of relaxation and freedom are the best thing for him. Yet it would seem that he is laying himself wide open to criticism unless he maintains a reasonable balance of activity and interest in both professional and personal matters.

If there are too many of this kind of fellow at one convention, the convention itself is sometimes liable to criticism.

A word to the young fellow who has just started going to meetings. You will see some "old-timers" who may be holding the attention of a group of people with their hilarity, story-telling, and general indulgence in a good time. Don't *you* try that yet. Those fellows have been coming to these meetings for a long time. Their records of service and work are well known. Everyone knows that they are fundamentally stable, even though they may be acting a little giddy just now. They can "get by with it." If you try it everyone will think that you are merely fresh and impertinent. Even the fellows whom you are trying to copy will not approve of you. Take your time and "go easy." It is better at this point to be a little too formal than to become too friendly in too short a time.

Just plain good manners should be the behavior theme for the young supervisor at a convention. How many young men have created bad impressions by beginning to call older supervisors by their first names too soon! How many young supervisors, both young men and young women, have made poor impressions by their endeavors to monopolize conversations and convince their elders that the younger generation is the smartest thing on the scene!

Certainly the young fellow who is just starting out will want to meet people at a convention. That is one of the principal reasons why he attends—to meet people and exchange ideas. He will have no trouble in doing it. It is a common occurrence at a convention for one to stop and talk with people whom he has never met. A question about the program, an inquiry regarding where a certain meeting is being held—any approach of this kind is sufficient to open a conversation which, if continued, may include a self-introduction. After all, this is a professional meeting, not a social function. Self-introductions are definitely proper and in order. But it must be remembered that self-introductions must be made in good taste and with good manners.

Now back to the programs. Let's not forget the programs. Of course an important part of the convention is the more informal life of the corridors and the lobbies. But a serious attitude toward the programs themselves is not to be placed in a secondary position even though we may hear people say "Oh, I come to these meetings because of the people I see, not because of the programs."

The smart supervisor keeps some adequate and accurate notes of the discussions and demonstrations which he attends. All of these things may be clear in his mind *now* but he wants a record of them for the basis of reports to be made later.

If we may be permitted to be generally critical at this point we will say that the listening habits of music educators are many times far from commendable. Why is it that the fellow who became so wrought up last week when two youngsters in the balcony made some noise during his chorus concert is now utterly unconcerned about the disturbance which he makes by moving around the fringe of the crowd in the convention auditorium and talking to his friends in a loud voice while one of his fellow supervisors is conducting a chorus on the stage? Why? We don't know. Music educators, of all people, should be good and quiet listeners.

The foregoing paragraphs may sound suspiciously like scolding. They are not so intended. The contentions in them cannot be dismissed as mere scolding. They are thoughts and ideas which have been expressed many times by a large number of music educators themselves. They are not merely the opinions, likes, and dislikes of the writer. He presents them frankly and seriously because he has seen the careers of some young music supervisors severely retarded by breaches of good taste and good manners—perhaps more often than by downright musical and professional incapability.

Reporting upon Meetings

What will Dale Haskins do when he goes home after a convention? Will he wait until his superintendent asks him about it before he makes any report? Or will he have in mind a definite plan through which he will make it apparent to everyone concerned that he obtained some real benefits from the meeting, benefits which he can pass on to the schools and to the community which pays his salary?

The first thing Dale should do is sit down and write out a rather complete report. Several copies of it should be given to his superintendent, who may pass some of them on to board of education members. Dale asked for permission to be absent from school for three days to attend a meeting. His superintendent backed his request and the board granted it. The least he can do is to provide them with a full report of the meeting and at the same time present some definite conclusions regarding ways and means through which he expects to better his work as a result of the new ideas which he got at the meeting.

At a teachers meeting Dale will probably be asked to make

a brief oral report. Knowing that the other teachers go to meetings, too, he will not bore them with a lot of generalizations. He will single out several principal ideas which are new and progressive and present them as interestingly as he can.

When Dale has good occasion to do so he will mention some of the new ideas to a few people around town and they will see that their schools will benefit as a result of his going to the convention. Those people will then be in position to make the right kind of reply if someone pops up with the question, "Why do they let these teachers run around the country to meetings on school time?"

Chapter 11

DEGREES AND LEARNING

A Preliminary Consideration

THE word "and" in the title "Degrees and Learning" is not capricious. It is not intended to convey the thought that degrees are without learning or the other way around. Rather it is our purpose to give objective consideration to two kinds of study: first, the kind which leads to the acquisition of college degrees; second, the kind which may be gathered in innumerable locations and situations remote from academic sponsorship.

For many decades after the introduction of music into the curriculum of the schools of the United States, music teachers and supervisors were certified in nearly all states upon a basis of requirements very different from those demanded of an applicant for an "academic" certificate. Musicians were trained as musicians and few of them studied liberal arts or professional education courses. On the other hand, the professional schools of education offered few or no courses having to do with music. How then could state certifying authorities ask applicants for music certificates to come to them with a combination of general academic education, professional educational training, and music training? It did not even occur to them to do so. It would have been out of the question.

Then there came the realization that *music* training alone was not sufficient for the person who wished to become a

148

teacher of music in the schools. The qualifications for music teaching certificates began their steady climb upward. Colleges, universities, and normal schools enlarged their music instruction facilities. Those conservatories and music schools which wished to train school music teachers began to offer courses which provided academic and educational backgrounds for their students.

In recent years there has been much discussion of the effects of newer certification requirements in the school music field. On one hand it is contended that so much study is now required in academic and educational subjects that music training itself is being neglected. On the other hand it is argued that it is now reasonable to expect music teachers to have a background of general education equal to that of teachers of other subjects and also that they must understand the content and the workings of the present-day curriculum if music is to be made an integral part of the curriculum.

There is good reason to support both of the foregoing viewpoints. If music continues its drive for recognition as a basic subject in the curriculum, as contrasted with being a mere furbelow or luxury, there is no doubt that the requirements for music education certification will extend even higher in all three phases—music, academic, and professional.

The most obvious answer to this problem is that the preliminary training period for music educators will be lengthened beyond four years. The present four-year period which is generally sufficient for certification is a rather strenuous experience for a youth just out of high school. The academic subject teachers are after him and are telling him that his cultural background will be inadequate unless he is well-grounded in the language arts, social sciences, science, etc. The education instructors tell him that he will be lost in the teaching profession unless he is well-informed regarding the history and principles of education, psychology, curriculum building, current educational trends, etc. Then come the music instructors, who ask him what good all these other things will do him in his music education work unless he knows music as such—theory, literature, applied techniques of instruments and voice, etc.

So, we find the undergraduate music education student being pulled in many directions at once. He would study his history tonight if he did not have to go to rehearsal for the opera which will be presented next week. His violin lesson would have been better today if he had not found it necessary to spend a lot of time during the past few days preparing for a history of education quiz which he took this morning. His French grades are dragging the ground. How can he do any really "creative" work in his composition class if he does not have time to sit down and get himself into some sort of mood in which he can develop some original ideas. His practice teaching is being done without sufficient preparation and he knows it. So it goes.

On top of all this the student is still a human being who has to have social life and recreation, not to speak of physical exercise on the tennis court, in the gymnasium, or somewhere else.

All this is a pretty large order, isn't it? What is the student to do? Nothing but make the best of it and hope that a lot of this training sticks for the future, but much of his "learning" is so superficial that it quickly disappears. The student jumps from one thing to another so often and so hurriedly that little of what he learns in one direction soaks in sufficiently to prevent it from being easily brushed off by some succeeding activity which suddenly takes over his mind and his energy.

Nor will it do any good if the undergraduate now sits back and presents an alibi for himself by saying, "See there! That's just what I've been contending. We have too much to do in the time at our disposal. If we did fewer things we could do them better." Everyone knows that. The instructors know it better than the students.

Perhaps in years to come the undergraduate period will be lengthened. Then life will become simpler and better ordered (if someone doesn't think up a lot of new courses in the meantime) and the learning will penetrate better. A student will not merely fiddle or toot his way through a lot of music in a hurried manner. He will have time to become really acquainted with the music, take it to himself and cherish it. His work in the social studies will not be merely that of cramming dates, names, places, and events. He will see the larger outlines and meanings of social, economic, and political themes. He will see their place in history and their relation to his present-day life. His education courses will take on a new meaning (now he sometimes wonders if they have any meaning at all) and he will begin to see that real mastery of general principles in education will be of value to him. His pace will be sufficiently deliberate that he can now and then put his knowledge of musical theory to work in some creative efforts. His study of the literature of music will become wider and at the same time more intensive and not be merely a consideration of the surface facts *about* the music to which he listens. He will have opportunity to learn the music itself.

All these advantages and more will accrue. His transition from a high school student to a professional teacher will be more gradual and more thorough. He will not merely grow older, he will ripen and mellow in the process. His philosophical outlook will be broader and more tolerant. He will have time to *live* with people and enjoy them rather than to look upon them simply as other members of a nine o'clock class or impersonal instructors in subjects. He will be able to spend more time out of doors and to take that kind of exercise which will be the finest sort of insurance for comfortable living in later years.

Sounds good, doesn't it? Also impossible just now? Perhaps so, but we believe that this kind of education is on the way. It must come if young music educators are going into the field with a broad cultural background which will serve as a sounding shell for their superior professional efforts. If nothing else will produce this kind of training, competition itself will eventually do so.

But at the moment we must be practical and look at the present set-up. The student starts his training with the idea that he and his family can afford four years and no more. Four years from now he must have a job and start earning money. Four years of a dizzy, rushing stream that pounds him first one way and then another and hardly lets him get a breath. Four years of a crazy quilt. He doesn't know its general design but he keeps pursuing all the strange and unmeaningful parts which somehow or other he must put together.

If you, the reader, are an undergraduate student do not for one moment think that you can explain all your shortcomings by merely setting forth arguments like the above. You have to face the facts as they are, not as we all hope they will be sometime.

Certainly these four years of training which you are now taking will not do for you all that this longer period would do. But you are not living in that future day; you are living today and you will have to realize to the utmost upon what you have at hand.

Through?

Now we come to a most important consideration for the young music educator of today. When you finish your four-year undergraduate training are you through learning?

If you continue your training will you know how to go about it?

Up to this point it has been taken for granted that your undergraduate work will secure for you a baccalaureate degree and will provide those courses which will be generally sufficient for certification as a school music teacher.

What about graduate study and other advanced learning fields?

What About Degrees?

The subject of degrees is highly debatable and there are many strongly conflicting opinions concerning it. It is also a somewhat dangerous subject but one which cannot be ignored in this discussion.

First, some generalizations. Degrees can be meaningful or they can be mere letters of the alphabet. Their value depends greatly upon the purpose of the student; it also depends greatly upon the integrity and standards of the institutions which grant them.

Some students work for advanced degrees in order to learn something; others work for advanced degrees merely to get advanced degrees.

Some of the most effective people in the music education field hold advanced degrees. The work which they did to secure them has contributed greatly to their professional growth and progress. Their degrees mean something.

Some of the most incompetent people in the field also have advanced degrees. They depend upon their degrees to do for them what they cannot do or will not do for themselves.

Most degrees do represent a successful completion of a certain amount of work and learning. Most institutions are at least reasonably rigid and high in their standards and requirements for advanced degrees.

The business of *getting* degrees just for the sake of *having* degrees has not been a particularly bright page in the recent history of American education. Degree getting has approached the proportions of a racket. Who is to blame? We don't know; it doesn't matter for our purposes here. What does matter is the fact that degree getting has in so many instances resulted in so little actual learning and advancement.

First, some blame must go to some of the students themselves. Even though they may have been forced through state or local requirements, salary schedule requirements, etc., to obtain advanced degrees, there is no justification for the resentful, lackadaisical, and uninterested attitude which some of them have taken toward further study. Any mind which does not respond positively and eagerly to more learning is hardly a mind which will be outstanding in its leadership of other minds.

Second, let us toss a brick in the direction of the colleges and universities. There have been instances in which the school authorities have required candidates for advanced degrees to enroll in courses which were of little or no value to them. Many students who have looked forward to graduate work as an exciting venture have found themselves shunted into a series of courses in which the content has been unsuited to their needs and interests. It is true that the college must have some supervision over the choice of courses leading to degrees, but it is also true that colleges have been known to "sell" courses in which the enrollment was too low for them to be profitable, much the same way that the green grocer attempts to sell his over-ripe strawberries on Saturday night.

A leading editorial by Karl W. Gehrkens in the October, 1940 *Music Educators Journal* states, "Too many graduate schools base their requirements on tradition rather than upon the needs of their students. Often the curriculum is merely thrown together, with no consideration for the student—or for anything else. . . . If . . . the music educator shall have a master's degree, it must be on the basis of the practicability of the work that is required for the degree."

Third, a prevalent grievance against graduate courses is that in many instances they are the same as *undergraduate* courses. Many times a class will be made up of both graduate and undergraduate students. The lectures and discussions are really on an undergraduate level. The only difference lies in the fact that the graduate students are required to do more outside reading and reference work. Students who enroll in graduate courses have every reason to expect that all members of the classes will be capable of advanced work and that the instructors will be capable of advanced teaching. Failure to meet these standards generally weakens the cause of graduate study except with those who are deliberately after degrees and want to get them the easiest and quickest way.

Purposeful Work for Degrees

The foregoing paragraphs have not been written merely for the purpose of criticizing graduate work in general. Rather, they are intended to convey to the reader the idea that a student who really wants to learn and who is entering upon graduate work should keep alert and take every precaution to insure his being enrolled in those courses which will best contribute to his growth. He should not start work toward an advanced degree until he knows where his real interests lie and has some definite idea of the kinds of courses which he wishes to take and the kind of work he wishes to do. If he does not know these things he is likely to find himself going through the mill just like any other machined product. When it is too late he will discover what has happened to him and probably will then give up in despair and figure that the best thing to do is to take the path of the least resistance—which is also the path of the least learning and progress.

It is well for anyone who wishes to enroll for graduate work to have one or two conferences with the proper authorities of the college which is under consideration before appearing for actual enrollment. Any person who wishes to work for a degree in such a way that the results will be of real value to him should be well-informed in advance concerning the channels of activity which will be open to him and the courses which will be required of him. He should also insist upon an evaluation of the work which he has presented for advanced standing so that there will be no misunderstanding later about credit allowances.

The purposeful candidate is going to *work* for his degree and *earn* it. The college is not going to *give* it to him. He should, then, have something to say about the building of a course which will give him maximum preparation for his work and plans in the years to come. The college has no right to throw a batch of courses of just any kind at him and say "Take it or leave it." He has some right to determine the direction, shape, and content of his further work.

If our concern about graduate study and degrees is tinged with agitation it is because of the all too prevalent opinion in the music education field that graduate work has as its primary purpose *degree getting* rather than serious and purposeful study.

There is no wish here to be unduly or unjustly critical of either students or institutions, but rather a desire to point out those elements which seem to contribute most to a truly unfortunate situation—one in which the members of the music education profession lack interest in and the most desirable kinds of attitudes toward and respect for graduate work as it has been offered in recent years. This situation must be greatly improved if music education is to be regarded as a real profession which can command the respect accorded other worth-while professions.

The young educator should seriously consider the possibilities of obtaining advanced degrees, for in most instances they represent real accomplishment. He should choose a school in which he has faith. That faith must extend to the director and the members of the department in which he will do his principal work. Once his arrangements are made and he is certain of his course ahead, he will find exciting and profitable experience in advanced study.

Advanced College Study—Not for Degrees

Some music educators, those who are not concerned with the matter of degree holding, have found it most advantageous to enroll for occasional courses in colleges in different parts of the country. By taking the classification of "special" students and signifying that they do not wish to become candidates for degrees they may enter many graduate courses.

If Homer Elwell has taken all of his courses to date at Central University it is a good idea for him to run out to Western University for a course or two—or to Southern University, Northern University, or Eastern University. He will meet new people, pick up some different ideas about music education, learn more about his country and its people, and find it a generally refreshing experience.

There is danger of stagnation in staying year after year with the same crowd, reworking the same old ideas in the same old way. New ideas are being brought forth in all parts of the country. Go take a look at some of them.

Many times a summer excursion railway ticket can provide both a new experience in schooling and a vacation trip.

Analyzing Needs for Study

Before enrolling for courses of any kind under any auspices, the student should have well in mind his deficiencies and his needs. If Homer Elwell needs to know more about woodwind instruments, let him look around and find the person or the school which can give him the best training. Perhaps he will wish to concentrate all his time and efforts for a while on the problem of woodwind instruments. He may later go to some other person or school for choral techniques training, or for fresh and interesting grade methods. He should not go to school just to take whatever courses are offered; he should go with a well-defined idea of his needs.

Study Outside Schools

One of the country's most noted bandmasters has studied with literally dozens of instrumental instructors. Whenever he is in a city where the symphony orchestra includes some man who is a particularly excellent teacher of some instrument this bandmaster takes one, two, three—as many lessons as he can while he is there. If some prominent instrumental organization which comes to his town includes some outstanding player, he goes to that man for as many lessons as he can arrange.

Then when this bandmaster does particularly brilliant instrumental instruction in a clinic, someone is certain to say, "It's just a gift to be able to know instruments as well as he does." Yes, it *is* a gift—a gift plus the will to do hard work.

There are thousands of competent musicians scattered throughout the country—instrumentalists, singers, composers, arrangers, etc. The music educator would not find many of them able to help him in his problems of group teaching, classroom management, and organization, but they can teach him about *music*. Too many music educators stop their study of *music* at an early date and devote all their further efforts to the *ways of teaching music*. This eventually produces musical sterility.

In years past, the music educator and the musician who lived and worked in the same town were inclined to regard each other with suspicion. That feeling is changing, and the smart music educator now avails himself of all possible assistance from the professional musician.

Studying Alone

Velma Mitchell has been told several times by her superintendent that the board of education thinks it might be best to replace her with a man instructor in order that the schools may have a better instrumental program. Velma is greatly disturbed and is wailing a lot about the injustice of it all. She says that she cannot afford to take a leave of absence and go in for a thorough study of instrumental instruction. She can go to one or two summer sessions, but she is smart enough to know that a few weeks spent on tooting first one instrument and then another for short periods of time will not make her into a capable instrumental teacher.

Is there any reason why Velma cannot do a lot of instrumental work by herself? Certainly she can borrow a clarinet and a cornet from someone and start working on them. She should have some lessons at first, and there surely are some good players of those instruments in reasonable distance who can give her lessons. There are many good instruction books which will do almost everything but pick up the instruments and play them for her. Then what is to prevent Velma's learning a lot about these two instruments during the next few months? Nothing except Velma's lack of will to do. She would surprise herself in what she could learn about a number of instruments in a year's time. Then some courses in instrumental instruction in summer school next year would put her in a fairly good position to start some instrumental work next fall.

Milton White has always insisted that he is interested in modern music and is so sorry he doesn't live in one of the large cities where he could hear a lot of it played. Well, if Milton would only spend a little time looking over radio programs he would be surprised how much of it he could "pipe" right into his living room at no cost. If he would spend only a few dollars a month on new recordings he would soon have a good library. Most of the facilities of the city will come out to Milton if he really wants them.

Much good studying alone can be done by any music educator. Radio, phonograph recordings, and sound films furnish music to the supervisor in the small desert town just as impartially and as effectively as they do to the city supervisor.

It is all a question of whether he really *wants* to learn. He will find the time and the energy if the desire is strong enough.

Not Only Music

The supervisor who wishes to be a generally intelligent and learned fellow will concern himself with things other than music. He will give some study and thought to the world about him. He will come to know more of its social, political, and economic problems. He will be interested in its scientific advancement. He will take a genuine interest in all the lively arts—not just music. New literature, new theatre, new graphic and plastic arts, new dance, new architecture—all these will engage his attention and keep him fresh in his interests.

Here is a supervisor who has been going to school for a long time—regular and summer sessions. All his courses have been for the purpose of training him as a music supervisor. Suddenly he decides that he is going to take a course in some other field, just for the fun of it. He moves into another sphere of interest which has nothing to do with music and music teaching. You can be certain that the "vacation" will do him and his music teaching a lot of good.

One of the heaviest liabilities in the music education field is the fellow who doesn't know how to talk about anything except music.

If we are going to insist that music have a larger place in living, then it would be well for every music educator to know a great deal about life.

Thinking

True scholarship and erudition are not the immediate or direct products of organized projects of learning—classes, lectures, assignments, theses, reports, and the like. These activities are productive of intelligence and learning. They provide the participant with experiences and precepts which he may use as the basis for his thinking.

Thinking, in the sense of creation and growth, comes when the individual sits down with himself, stirs around these precepts and experiences in his mind, examines them, re-evaluates them, fits them together, pulls them apart, discards them, brings them back, makes new patterns of them, discards the new patterns, and so on and on until there comes a new pattern which is meaningful. It is a new idea. It is a contribution to existent knowledge.

How does all this happen? We do not know and will not attempt to explain. But it does happen.

But merely to conform well, to copy other people's procedures, to do their ways of doing as well as they—all of these things are not *thinking*! They are merely imitation supported by skill.

Let's not confuse thinking with intelligence and learning. Knowledge may be acquired and learning achieved in a somewhat mechanical manner. But *thinking* is an essentially creative and productive process.

Let us not picture the "thinker" as a person who remains apart from the world and the experiences which it offers. He does not reside constantly in beautiful surroundings, soft lights, and a hushed atmosphere suggestive of the crystal gazer. He is more likely to be a fellow who has taught classes all day and now feels pretty much discouraged about the whole business. Nothing seemed to be right. Music did not do for the pupils what he wanted it to do. Was it the fault of the music, of the children, or of his own endeavors? What is the trouble?

He begins to check his list. What did he do? What did he leave undone? More checking. Some rejections. Some additions. The whole thing still does not make sense. Professor So-and-So used to say this or that. On the other hand someone else said the opposite. These things do not fit together. Suppose . . . No, that wouldn't do. Well, then, suppose . . . No, that wouldn't do, either. But if you take this and put it with that . . . Yes, that looks more like the shape of an idea. Add this, then. Now the pattern takes on line and form. Add this. Now it has color. The picture is complete and he has never seen it before. Perhaps no one else has, either.

A good picture? A true picture? Will it last? Will it keep the meaning which seems so clear now? He doesn't know. No one knows. But he has a new idea to try. Time and use will take care of the rest.

Do music educators really think through the problems and developments of their work? Or do they justify their procedures in the light of writings and speakings of other people?

Tens of thousands of people have been engaged in music education in this country during recent decades. Read the literature of music education, examine its findings, note the strong influences which have been outstanding and you will come to the conclusion that the real thinking has come from very few minds. Accomplishment of standards in performance, acquisition of skills, intelligent application of recognized procedures—all of these can be placed to the credit of many successful teachers and supervisors.

But what about *thinking*?

Is there any reason why the young music educator should not begin his thinking right off? Certainly not. He will carry on his work with a high regard for the things which have been taught to him. He will do well to follow those precepts which have been given to him during his years of training. But if he ever expects to make a contribution to music education other than skilled conformity, he will begin to *think* at once.

He will question everything that he does. He will question in the spirit of searching for truth, not merely as an agnostic and smart-aleck questioner. He will constantly evaluate the quality of the music which serves as the stuff of his teaching program. He will watch carefully his procedures and methods to see that they are effective. He will watch the reactions of his students to make certain that music is doing something to and for them.

His should be no life of complete dependence upon previously prepared lists of music to be taught and notebooks of methods to be used, with willingness to follow without question those lines of procedure which others have developed. He will use all these contributions as effectively as possible, and be grateful for them. But they will form a base for his departure to find all possible ways, his own and other people's, to increase the value and meaning of his work.

Writing

Where is the person who does not think that he has some really good ideas once in a while? He doesn't exist. But what does the average fellow do about his ideas? Generally, nothing. Why? Because he forgets about them. What should he do about them? Write them down as soon as he has them.

Why? Because he can then sit down some day with those notes and go into a thinking session and come out with something worth while.

Suppose that he does bring forth some ideas which look promising, what should he do then? The first thing to do is put them into action in his own teaching program and see what happens.

Suppose they work out well in practice, what then? He should put them in shape so that they will be available to others in the profession. He should be articulate on paper.

There is great need in the music education field for better quality in the writing of articles, papers, and books. Much truly valuable material is lost to a large percentage of readers because it mires down in a heavy marsh of meaningless words and styleless writing.

Certainly it would be unfair to expect music educators to be possessed of a quality of style comparable to that of professional writers. However, as we read the professional writings of music education we believe that they could be greatly improved if the writers would give a little additional time and effort to perfection of writing technique.

It is largely a matter of work and thought rather than dependence upon a natural flair for writing. Do ideas seem to be unfolding in proper sequence? No? Well then, let's shift them around. Is there clarity of thought? No. What shall we do? First, let's re-evaluate our words. Do we have those words which best express what we have to say? If not, the dictionary or thesaurus will help. Are they in their proper places, or do they seem jumbled? Let's change them around several times and see if we come out with better results. Perhaps we shall discard a few words in the process. And so on and on until we think we have done our best.

Now let's put this piece of writing aside for a time and come back to it later. We read it and wonder how we were ever able to write anything so poor. So we throw the whole thing away and start all over, taking a new kind of approach.

This simple but tedious business of keeping at the job in writing is much more likely to be fruitful of results than a high-powered concentrated course.

The person who is doing the writing should not think of his output in terms of publication value. He should regard the whole process as one of thought development and clarification. Then when he becomes proficient and really has something to say the publication angle will take care of itself.

Will the reader please answer one question? Why is so much "educational" writing devoid of a real human interest flavor and sense of humor? Why? It's a mystery!

Chapter 12

CREDO

So here are many pages which deal with the everyday life and work of the average music supervisor in the average community. Take exception if you will to any of the questions raised and the suggestions given. They are general in nature as they must be in a consideration of the relation of thousands of music educators to millions of citizens. Exceptions are granted, as are omissions. After all, music education is not a formula. It has no objective and impersonal set of rules and regulations which may be applied to its proponents, its procedures, and its products.

We have discussed many of the more practical problems of the music teacher. And, by the way, we *do* like the term "teacher" better than "supervisor" or "educator." The three have been used somewhat interchangeably in this text. But, *teaching* must remain the soul of the whole business, otherwise there will result a mechanical process of organization and management of a superficial nature.

Now here is a teacher who looks as if he has all the necessary qualifications. May we describe him in brief phrases? Good general education. Pleasing personality. Good musician. Knows how to get jobs. Knows how to ingratiate himself into the life of a community. Excellent instructor. Knows business procedures, organization, and management. Dresses and appears well. Has fine professional standing and relationships. Has always made an excellent impression in public and press.

Say! This fellow looks just like what we have been asking for. He *knows* the right things. He *acts* the right way. He *does* the right things. What more can we ask of him? PLENTY.

Now comes the time when we have to go inside this fellow and find out why he is in music education. That is the most important thing of all.

Is he here because he does not know what else to do?

Is he here because he thinks that music teachers make better than average salaries?

Is he here because he thinks that his exterior qualities will be sufficient for his success?

Is he here because he has been frustrated in some other music activity?

If he answers "Yes" to any of these questions he should be made to realize that he is cheating himself and many other people.

While *he* is of less importance than the children and adult citizens involved, let's consider his problem first. He's cheating himself because he will not put into his work those spiritual and emotional values which make the difference between a humdrum, casual, and static life and a life which is crammed with zestful adventure, joy of accomplishment, and a realization that his efforts can make a meaningful contribution to a finer, deeper life for those people with whom he comes into contact. The teacher who has found his groove in making people feel and live differently because of music is one who can walk with pride and who can carry with him a deep, quiet satisfaction. And, do not mistake our use of the word "groove"—we do not mean a narrow, unchanging pathway. Far from it.

And now what about the other people involved? Is "school

music" going to mean to them a spiritual and emotional unfolding, or is it going to be a mechanical routine of lines, spaces, sharps, flats, third fingers, quarter notes, tonic chords, and information about the lives of composers? It will be the latter if the teacher is "on the surface." It cannot be anything else if his interest lies in the teaching of surface facts and techniques. Yes, he may develop skill and knowledge. But what of it? It will be a hard, brittle process which will prevent the participants' actual absorption into the meaning of the music itself. Then what do you have? Merely a graveyard of factual bones. And that is not MUSIC!

A true love for music, an impulse to cherish music, a realization of the power of music in spiritual growth—all of these must be a part of him who would bring music to others. And, too, he must assume his title of *teacher* with an attitude of greatest respect for its many implications.

So, far above all these practical considerations of daily routines with their many troublesome and puzzling moments must stand the music teacher's implicit faith in music, his faith in music as an important part of the spiritual life of the individual and the nation.

Without that faith the mechanics of procedure mean nothing.

Appendix

Appendix

NATIONAL ASSOCIATION OF TEACHERS AGENCIES

CALIFORNIA

Frankford Pacific Teachers Agency, 531 Stack Bldg., Los Angeles.

COLORADO

Rocky Mountain Teachers Agency, 410 U. S. National Bank Bldg., Denver.

Western Teachers Exchange, 752 Gas and Electric Bldg., Denver.

CONNECTICUT

Cary Teachers Agency, 49 Pearl St., Hartford.

ILLINOIS

Albert Teachers Agency, 25 East Jackson Blvd., Chicago.

Clark–Brewer Teachers Agency, 64 East Jackson Blvd., Chicago.

Fisk Teachers Agency, 28 East Jackson Blvd., Chicago.

Hughes Teachers Agency, 25 East Jackson Blvd., Chicago.

Illiana Teachers Agency, Champaign.

IOWA

Clinton Teachers Agency, Clinton.

Midland Schools Teachers Agency, 312 Flynn Bldg., Des Moines.

Sabins' Educational Exchange, 411 Shops Bldg., Des Moines.

MAINE

New England Teachers Agency, 10 Congress St., Portland.

MASSACHUSETTS

Grace M. Abbott Teachers Agency, 120 Boylston St., Boston.

American Teachers Agency, 30 Albemarle St., Springfield.

Cary Teachers Agency, 14 Beacon St., Boston.

Fickett Teachers Agency, 8 Beacon St., Boston.

Fisk Teachers Agency, 120 Boylston St., Boston.

174 MORE THAN A PITCH-PIPE

MICHIGAN
Detroit Teachers Agency, 1101 Park Ave., Detroit.

MINNESOTA
Clark-Brewer Teachers Agency, 509 Palace Bldg., Minneapolis.
Schummers School Service, 813 Lumber Exchange, Minneapolis.
Western Teachers Exchange, Plymouth Bldg., Minneapolis.

MISSOURI
Clark-Brewer Teachers Agency, New York Life Bldg., Kansas City.
Specialists Educational Bureau, 302 Olivia Bldg., St. Louis.

MONTANA
E. L. Huff Teachers Agency, 1222 Helen Ave., Missoula.

NEBRASKA
Davis School Service, 675 Stuart Building, Lincoln.

NEW YORK
Allied Teachers Agency, 500 Fifth Ave., New York.
American & Foreign Teachers Agency, 19 West 44 St., New York.
Bardeen-Union Teachers Agency, 332 South Warren St., Syracuse.
Clark-Brewer Teachers Agency, Flatiron Bldg., New York.
Co-operative Teachers Agency, Hurst Bldg., Buffalo.
Interstate Teachers Agency, 533 Genesee Valley Trust Bldg., Rochester.
Kellogg Teachers Agency, 31 Union Square, New York.
Pratt Teachers Agency, 70 Fifth Ave., New York.
Schermerhorn Teachers Agency, 366 Fifth Ave., New York.

NORTH DAKOTA
Love Teachers Agency, Huntington Block, Fargo.

OHIO
Ohio Midland Teachers Agency, Chamber of Commerce Bldg., Columbus.
Schermerhorn Teachers Agency, 1836 Euclid Ave., Cleveland.

OREGON
Northwest Teachers Association, 812 Guardian Bldg., Portland.

PENNSYLVANIA

Bryant Teachers Bureau, 711 Witherspoon Bldg., Philadelphia.
Central Teachers Agency, 202 Walnut St., Harrisburg.
Great American Teachers Agency, 205 N. Seventh St., Allentown.

SOUTH CAROLINA

Southern Teachers Agency, Columbia.

SOUTH DAKOTA

Bersagel Teacher Service, 417 Citizens Bank Bldg., Aberdeen.
National Teachers Exchange, Sioux Falls.

TENNESSEE

College & Specialist Bureau, Goodwyn Institute Bldg., Memphis.
Southern Teachers Agency, Hamilton Natl. Bank Bldg., Chattanooga.

UTAH

Yergensen Teachers Agency, 939 S. 12th East, Salt Lake City.

VIRGINIA

Southern Teachers Agency, Broad–Grace Arcade, Richmond.

WASHINGTON

Clark–Brewer Teachers Agency, Columbia Bldg., Spokane.
Westmore Teachers Agency, Old National Bank Bldg., Spokane.

WISCONSIN

Parker Teachers Agency, 518 Beaver Ins. Bldg., Madison.

JAMES McARTHUR

Home address: 221 Pine Ridge Road, Winton, N. J. Telephone: Winton 196J.

Present address: 141 Horton Avenue, Fairview, Pa. Telephone: Fairview 8473.

Age: 22. Height: 5' 10". Weight: 165 pounds. Church affiliation: Methodist.

General education:
  High School, Winton, N. J. Graduated 1934.
  Union Teachers College, Arlington, Pa. B.S. in Ed., 1938.
  Metropolitan University, New York, N. Y. Two summer terms, 1939 and 1940.

Professional education:
  Union Teachers College: Degree noted above with major in music education. Courses included: applied study of piano, voice, violin, cornet, and clarinet; ear-training; sight-reading; harmony; counterpoint; history of music; music appreciation; methods, vocal and instrumental, high school and elementary; conducting. Also courses in psychology, principles of education, and history of education.
  Metropolitan University: Graduate courses in instrumental methods, high school methods, harmony, psychology of music, voice, and violin.
  Six years of violin study with Emil Weishausen of the Philadelphia Orchestra.
  Three years of private theory and composition study with Ernest Martin.

176

Professional experience:
Two years as supervisor of music in Fairview, Pa., including all vocal and instrumental work from first grade through high school.

Activities:
Four years in Winton High School band and boys glee club.
Leading parts in high school operettas.
Extensive experience in Union Teachers College band, orchestra, and choir.
Violin soloist at several college concerts.
Composed the music for a senior class show at college.
Active in affairs of Current Events Club and College Co-Op Association.
Member of Music Educators National Conference and State Teachers Association.
Member of Phi Lambda Mu, honorary professional music fraternity.
Vice-president of college Student Government Association.

References:
Mr. W. L. Carter, high school principal, Winton, N. J.
Mr. H. W. Benningham, head of music department, Union Teachers College.
Mr. Roland W. Storrs, superintendent of schools, Fairview, Pa.
Rev. Barton McCune, pastor of Methodist church, Winton, N. J.